THE SQUEEZE AT BRIDGE

CADOGAN BRIDGE SERIES

Publishing Editor: Glyn Liggins

In this series:

REESE, T.
Brillancies and Blunders
in the European Bridge Championship

FLINT, J. & NORTH, F.
Tiger Bridge Revisited

REESE, T. & BIRD, D.
Famous Hands from Famous Matches

SMITH, N.
Bridge Literature

SENIOR, B.
Bread & Butter Bidding

In Preparation:

CROWHURST, E.
Acol – The Complete System

RIGAL, B.
Test your Bridge Judgement

For a complete catalogue of Cadogan Bridge Books (which includes the former
Maxwell Macmillan Bridge list) please write to:

Cadogan Books, 369 Euston Road, London NW1 3AR
Tel: (071) 388 2404 Fax: (071) 388 2407

THE SQUEEZE AT BRIDGE

by

CHIEN-HWA WANG

CADOGAN BRIDGE

LONDON, NEW YORK

CADOGAN BOOKS DISTRIBUTION

UK/EUROPE/AUSTRALASIA/ASIA/AFRICA
Distribution: Grantham Book Services Ltd, Isaac Newton Way, Alma Park Industrial
Estate, Grantham, Lincs NG31 9SD
Tel: (0476) 67421 Fax: (0476) 590223

USA/CANADA/LATIN AMERICA/JAPAN
Distribution: Macmillan Distribution Centre, Front & Brown Streets, Riverside, New
Jersey 08075, U.S.A.
Tel: (609) 461 6500 Fax: (609) 764 9122

1993 Chien-Hwa Wang

Library of Congress Cataloguing-in-Publication Data
(applied for)

British Library Cataloguing in Publication Data
A CIP catalogue record for this book is available from the British Library

ISBN 1 85744 507 4

Cover by Stefron Graphics
Printed in Great Britain by BPCC Wheatons Ltd, Exeter

CONTENTS

Chapter 1

Elements of the Squeeze

1.1 Preliminaries

In bridge there is a large class of endplay in which a player, by leading a card in a suit, forces an opponent to discard in the other two or more guarded suits. Subsequently, the player and his partner take advantage of the forced discard and gain an extra trick for their side. In this case the endplay is called a squeeze. The opponent who is forced to surrender a guard in a suit is said to be squeezed. The card on the lead of which the opponent is squeezed is called a squeeze-card.

Before going further let us study this end position:

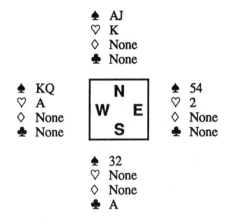

```
              ♠ AJ
              ♡ K
              ◇ None
              ♣ None

  ♠ KQ          N          ♠ 54
  ♡ A                       ♡ 2
  ◇ None    W     E         ◇ None
  ♣ None        S           ♣ None

              ♠ 32
              ♡ None
              ◇ None
              ♣ A
```

South is on lead in a no-trump contract.

South has two sure winners, but he can win all the three remaining tricks. South plays the ace of clubs, and West, who guards both the spade and the heart suits, is in trouble. If West discards a spade, North lets go of the king of hearts and wins the last two tricks with the ace and jack of spades. If West discards the ace of hearts, North lets go of the jack of spades and wins the last two tricks with the ace of spades and the king of hearts.

In this situation it is clear that West is squeezed on the lead of the ace of clubs, which is the squeeze-card.

The meaning of a squeeze being understood, we enter upon the fundamental requirements of a squeeze.

Firstly, it is obvious that the opponent to be squeezed must hold protection in at least two suits: spades and hearts in the above example. An opponent guarding only one suit can never be squeezed.

The fact that an opponent guards two suits means exactly that he is threatened in these suits. In the above example West is threatened with the jack of spades and the king of hearts. North's king of hearts is called a one-card menace against West's ace, and North's ace-jack of spades is a two-card menace against West's king-queen of spades. At least two menaces must be present in a squeeze position.

Secondly, the necessity of the presence of a squeeze-card is too evident to require explanation. If there is no squeeze-card, the opponent who guards two suits has nothing to do but to follow suit, and surely he will not present you with an undeserved extra trick.

However, a few words can be said about the nature of a squeeze-card. At first sight it might appear that a squeeze-card should be a winner to the player whose side executes the squeeze. In the majority of cases this is true, but in some rare cases it is not. In certain squeeze positions the squeeze-card can be a definite loser. This happens when a loser is conceded to a high card held by one opponent, while the other opponent is squeezed at the very same trick.

Some bridge authors have declined to use the term "squeeze" to describe those endplays such as one which combines a forcing discard with a trick-establishing play.

We call an endplay a squeeze whenever the play of a card forces an opponent to unguard a suit, thus enabling us to set up an extra winner. It can be a 'pure' squeeze of one opponent in two suits; it can be a combination of two squeezes, one against each opponent; it can also be a forcing discard which paves the way for a subsequent play that deprives the opponents of a vital trick. In each case we call it a squeeze. It makes no difference whether the gain of the extra trick is immediate or delayed. We observe that it will be safe to say that a squeeze-card must be a card in a suit in which the opponent squeezed is void. In cases when a squeeze against one opponent is followed by a squeeze against the other (as was pointed out in the preceding paragraph, this combination is called a squeeze), there are, in effect, two squeeze-cards.

The opponents need not both be void in the same suit; the situation can even be such that two squeezes operate successively, one against each opponent, and each opponent is squeezed on the lead of a winner in a suit that the other opponent guards.

Thirdly, at the moment the squeeze-card is led, the opponent to be squeezed should not have any useless card to discard. In other words, all his cards must be busy. In the above example West has no idle cards* left. He is squeezed because he lacks the room to retain guards in both suits.

This does not imply that the squeezing side must be able to win all but one of the remaining tricks, as might easily be misconstrued. However, this is true in the majority of cases, particularly with the comparatively simple squeezes.

In some other cases, for example, when a squeeze of an opponent is followed by another squeeze against the same opponent, the "all-but-one" condition is not satisfied.

Fourthly, the problem of entry is probably the most important in the squeeze. Even if all the other conditions are fulfilled, the squeeze still fails when necessary entries are not available.

Suppose, in the above end position, the ace of spades has been played earlier, then the situation would be this:

* The terms "busy" and "idle" were first used by Ely Culbertson.

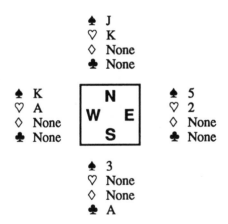

South to lead at no-trumps.

The first, second, and third conditions are all fulfilled: West is threatened in two suits (the jack of spades and king of hearts are menaces against West's king of spades and ace of hearts, respectively); South has a squeeze-card (the ace of clubs); all West's cards are busy. Yet there is no squeeze. On the lead of the ace of clubs, West can safely discard the ace of hearts without conceding an extra trick. The reason is that the North hand cannot be entered to cash the king of hearts, although it has become a winner after West's discard.

It may be convenient to introduce here the notions of "positional" and "automatic" squeezes.

Suppose a squeeze-card is led from the South hand. If North's choice of discards is dependent on West's discard, we say that the squeeze is *positional*. It follows that a positional squeeze will never operate against the wrong opponent, for North will have to part with a busy card before that opponent.

In the end position given at the beginning of this section the squeeze is effective mainly because West is forced to part with a busy card before North. It is a positional squeeze against West.

The squeeze fails if the East and West hands are interchanged:

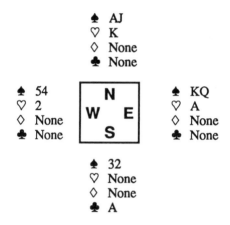

In this case East guards the two suits. If there is any squeeze it must be against East. South leads the ace of clubs, and North must discard before East. East will discard in whichever suit North lets go, and South cannot gain an extra trick.

To ensure a successful squeeze against either opponent it is necessary that there be room in the North hand for an idle card which can be thrown freely on the lead of the squeeze-card. In the above diagram the transfer of the one-card menace from North to South will bring this about:

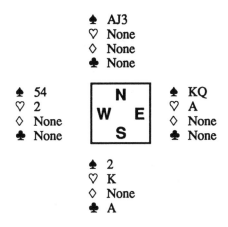

♠ AJ3
♡ None
◇ None
♣ None

♠ 54
♡ 2
◇ None
♣ None

♠ KQ
♡ A
◇ None
♣ None

♠ 2
♡ K
◇ None
♣ A

On the lead of the ace of clubs, North has an idle card to throw—the three of spades, and East is squeezed. If East discards a spade, North wins two spade tricks. If East discards the heart, South makes a heart and North a spade.

This squeeze is clearly more valuable than the one shown earlier. Either West or East, holding the only guards in the two suits, will be squeezed. We call such a squeeze an *automatic* squeeze, which is defined as a squeeze that works against either opponent.

These examples show that by the entries for a squeeze we mean not only the presence of these entries but also that they must be properly situated.

In various squeeze positions the requirements for entries are not always the same. We shall not endevour to give an elaborate description of the entry conditions in a squeeze; for, however elaborate it may be, it will not cover all the possibilities.

For the moment we only stress that entries necessary for the squeeze must be available.

Summing up: A squeeze is an endplay that forces an opponent to discard from guarded suits and sooner or later gains a trick for the player who performs this endplay. In performing a squeeze there must be a squeeze-card and at least two menaces, the opponent to be squeezed must hold nothing but busy cards, and whatever entries needed must be available.

1.2 Classification of menaces

Since the presence of menaces is essential in squeeze, and since the classification of squeezes will depend mainly on menaces, we shall, in the next section, make a full description of various types of menace.

The single menace

The simplest type of menace is the single menace, i.e. menace against one opponent:

The king of spades is a one-card single menace against West's ace. If West discards the ace, the king becomes a winner. East may have some spades, but they are all worthless.

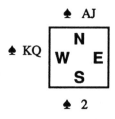

The ace-jack in the North hand is a two-card single menace against West. A two-card single menace is merely a one-card single menace plus an additional master card in the suit.

A two-card single menace often (though not always) needs a small card in the opposite hand so as to ensure an entry, as is shown in the last diagram.

In each of these diagrams, if the East-West cards are interchanged, the North-South combination is called a single menace against East.

Similarly we can form a three-card single menace, etc.

Single menaces will often be referred to simply as menaces.

The North-South cards in the next two diagrams are called split two-card single menaces against West:

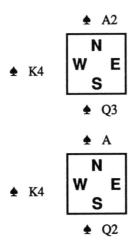

In both cases the queen is the menace card. In the first diagram, if West is forced to discard the four of spades, North can win with the ace and immediately return the two to South's queen. In the second diagram, if West discards the four, North plays the ace and has to cross to the South hand through a side entry in order to cash the queen.

Split three-card single menaces are shown in the next two diagrams:

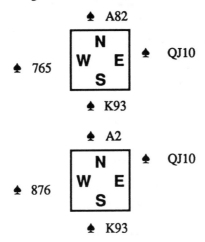

These are split three-card menaces against East. In the first diagram either the nine or the eight serves as menace card against East; in the second diagram the nine of spades is the menace card.

Occasionally in a squeeze situation, the presence of a menace of the following type is indispensable:

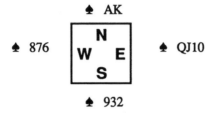

The nine of spades is the menace card against East. This combination of the North-South cards may also be described as a split three-card menace. In this diagram the two master cards are both in the North hand, as distinguished from the preceding ones where they are divided between North and South.

Another type of single menace is shown as follows:

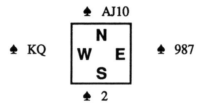

The North-South combination is known as an extended two-card menace against West. Without North's ten, the combination is an ordinary two-card menace against West. The ten is an additional card which, together with the jack, will be set up if West discards a spade. This type of menace occurs in some of the repeated squeezes.

Two lower-ranking cards of a suit also form a menace if one opponent only holds two master cards in the suit:

If West discards a spade, North leads the queen, losing to West's last good spade but setting up the jack as a winner. The queen-jack may be called an extended one-card menace against West's ace-king.

8

West's winners need not be both in the spade suit:

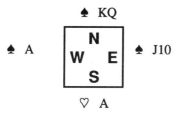

North's spade holding is again an extended one-card menace against West. If West can be forced to discard on the ace of hearts, the king of spades will be led to West's ace, and later North will make a spade trick with the queen.

Similarly, we have

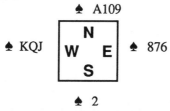

The North-South combination is an extended two-card menace against West. If West discards a spade, North can either duck a spade to West and later win two spade tricks, or first win the ace and then concede a spade to West, establishing the third spade trick.

It can be seen that the extended menace occurs only in squeeze situations where the "all-but-one" condition is not satisfied.

The double menace

A menace against both opponents is called a double menace.

The queen is a one-card menace against West's ace, and also a one-card menace against East's king. It is a one-card double menace. We observe that the queen will become a winner only if West and East both unguard the suit.

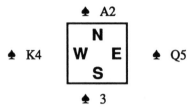

This is a two-card double menace. The two of spades is the menace card against both opponents.

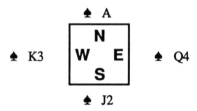

This combination of the North-South cards is called a split two-card double menace.

Similarly, the North-South combination in each of the next three diagrams is a split three-card double menace:

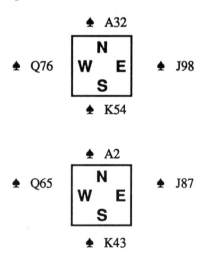

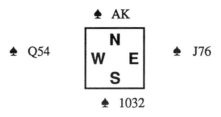

♠ AK

♠ Q54   ♠ J76

♠ 1032

In the first of these diagrams either North's three or South's five may be used as a menace card; in the second and third diagrams the menace card lies in the South hand.

Extended single menaces have their analogues in the double menace:

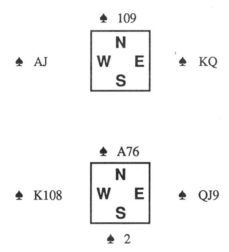

♠ 109

♠ AJ   ♠ KQ

♠ A76

♠ K108   ♠ QJ9

♠ 2

These are called extended one-card and two-card double menaces respectively. In each case, if both West and East discard a spade, a spade winner can be set up for North-South by first conceding a trick in that suit.

In all the double menaces given so far the menace card becomes a winner only if both opponents discard in the suit.

In the next diagram both opponents are threatened in a suit, while neither opponent can discard in it without conceding a trick.

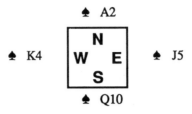

If West discards the four, North wins the ace and South the queen. If East discards the five, South leads the queen, and West must cover. The ace wins, felling East's lone jack, and the ten becomes a winner. This combination may be called a pick-up double menace.

Another pick-up double menace is shown as follows:

If West discards the two, the ten is led. West must win and the king is established. If East discards a spade, the king is led, felling East's now lone honour in spades and ensuring South of a spade trick. It should be noted that when a squeeze situation contains such a menace a trick is lost after the forcing discard.

It may be necessary, for the sake of completeness, to introduce this strange menace:

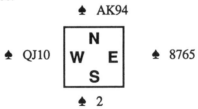

West is threatened with the nine and East with the four of spades. If West discards a spade, North wins three tricks in spades; and if East also discards a spade, North wins all four spade tricks. This double menace occurs in a unique situation in the repeated squeeze.

More advanced double menaces will be classified under other headings (see below).

The ruffing menace

Consider this diagram:

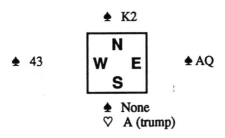

♠ K2

♠ 43

♠ AQ

♠ None
♡ A (trump)

If East discards the queen of spades, the two of spades is led and ruffed by South, and the king is established.

North's king-two of spades is called a two-card single ruffing menace against East's ace-queen. The term "single" refers to the fact that it is a menace against one opponent.

A three-card single ruffing menace is shown in the next diagram:

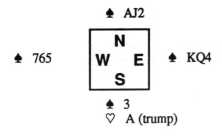

♠ AJ2

♠ 765

♠ KQ4

♠ 3
♡ A (trump)

This is a single ruffing menace against East, with an entry in the suit in the North hand. If East discards a spade, the ace of spades is cashed and the two led and ruffed, and the jack becomes a winner.

This menace is seldom of value because the ace-jack in the North hand, when used as an ordinary two-card menace against

East's king-queen, is often sufficient to produce an extra trick in a squeeze.

Here is another three-card ruffing menace:

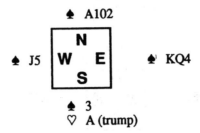

This diagram differs only slightly from the preceding one. But this time the ace-ten in the North hand no longer serves as an ordinary two-card single menace against East, for West also guards the suit. Now the presence of the trump suit becomes essential; if East can be forced to discard a spade, the ten of spades becomes a winner after the ace is cashed and the two led and ruffed. West's spade suit is one card shorter than North's and so West is unable to guard the third round.

Since West also partially guards the spade suit, strictly speaking this menace is not a single menace. We may call it a semi-double menace, but for simplicity we shall still refer to it as a three-card single ruffing menace against East.

Similar to what has been mentioned with regard to single menaces, single ruffing menaces will be referred to simply as ruffing menaces.

A double ruffing menace is a menace of such a nature that neither opponent can discard in the suit without enabling a trick to be ruffed out.

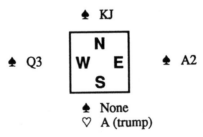

North's spade suit is a two-card double ruffing menace. If East discards the two of spades, the jack is led and ruffed, setting up the king. If West discards the three of spades, a ruffing-finesse position is established: North leads the king which East has to cover and South ruffs. At the same time West's queen falls and the jack becomes top in the suit.

This menace is somewhat similar in nature to a pick-up menace already described, but here the trump suit plays a vital role.

An analogous three-card menace is this:

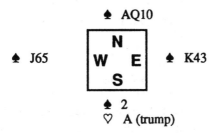

This is a three-card double ruffing menace, with an entry in the suit in the North hand. If East discards a spade, the ace is cashed and the ten led and ruffed, establishing the queen. If West discards a spade, North plays the ace and then the queen of spades, felling West's jack. Either the queen wins or the ten is ruffed out, depending on East's play.

The guard menace

It may happen that an opponent has to retain a card in a suit to guard his partner from a finesse position:

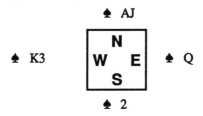

In this case East cannot afford to discard the lone queen, lest South leads the two and finesses the jack if West plays low. The North-South combination in this diagram is known as a two-card guard menace against East. It can be seen that a guard menace is also a double menace.

This is a split three-card guard menace against West. If West discards the six, the king drops the jack and a finesse can be taken against East's queen.

The clash menace

There is one more type of menace to be described:

West's singleton king will clash with South's queen on the lead of North's ace, and East can guard the second round of spades. Yet West cannot afford to discard the king lest North-South make the queen and ace separately. This combination of the North-South cards threatens both opponents: the queen is a menace card to West, while the two is a menace card to East. I termed it a clash menace in 1954. It is a two-card clash menace against West. Here the longer part of the clash menace lies over the opponent who is clash-menaced.

If the East-West cards are interchanged, we obtain a clash menace against East:

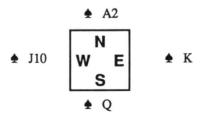

Now the longer part of the clash menace lies in front of East who is the clash-menaced opponent.

Like menaces of other types, a clash menace can be of three-card length and split:

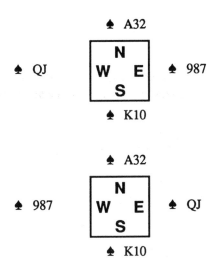

These are split three-card clash menaces against West and East, respectively. In the first diagram the longer part of the menace lies over the opponent clash-menaced; in the second it lies in front of the opponent clash-menaced. In both cases, if the clash-menaced opponent discards a spade, the king, ten and ace of spades will be made in turn.

1.3 Classification of squeezes

All the squeezes fall into two groups: the single squeeze in which only one opponent is forced to unguard a suit, and the double squeeze in which both opponents suffer this fate.

This is only a general classification. We proceed to give a more detailed classification of squeezes according to the types of menaces with which they are connected.

1. Simple squeeze. This is the simplest form of the squeeze being the squeeze of one opponent in two suits. All the menaces involved should be ordinary single menaces.

17

2. Double squeeze. A double squeeze is a combination of two simple squeezes, one against each opponent. The menaces involved should be single or double menaces, excluding any of the ruffing, guard and clash menaces.

3. Triple squeeze. A triple squeeze is a squeeze of one opponent in three suits. This kind of squeeze offers one and only one extra trick if the opponent squeezed discards correctly. The menaces involved are the same as those in a single or a double squeeze.

4. Repeated squeeze. A repeated squeeze is a squeeze of one opponent in three suits, through which the squeezing side can gain two extra tricks. A double repeated squeeze is a combination of a triple squeeze against one opponent and a simple squeeze against the other.

5. Ruffing squeeze. A ruffing squeeze is a squeeze in which one of the menaces is a ruffing menace. If only one opponent is squeezed, the squeeze is a single ruffing squeeze; and if both opponents are squeezed, it is a double ruffing squeeze. This kind of squeeze does not contain a guard menace or clash menace.

6. Guard squeeze. A guard squeeze is a squeeze of an opponent in three suits in one of which he is guard-menaced. The guard squeeze will be classified as single or double according to whether one or both opponents are involved in the squeeze. The menaces should not be clash menaces.

7. Clash squeeze. A clash squeeze is a squeeze of an opponent in three suits in one of which he is clash-menaced. If only one opponent is squeezed, and the menaces besides the clash menace are ordinary single menaces, it is a single clash squeeze. If both opponents are squeezed, and if one of the menaces besides the clash menace is a double menace, it is a double clash squeeze. If one of the menaces is a ruffing menace, it is a ruffing clash squeeze. Ruffing clash squeezes are subdivided into two classes, single and double, in the usual sense. If one opponent is guard-squeezed and the other clash-squeezed, the squeeze is called a guard clash squeeze.

Chapter 2

Simple Squeezes

2.1 The four fundamental forms

The simple squeeze is the easiest of all squeezes. An opponent is squeezed in two suits and is forced to discard a busy card in one of the two guarded suits. The declarer then takes advantage of the discard to gain an extra trick for his side.

Let us examine the following hand.

```
         ♠ A654
         ♡ K832
         ◇ K93
         ♣ 74

         ♠ QJ
         ♡ AQ5
         ◇ AQJ2
         ♣ J983
```

South	North
1NT	2♣
2◇	3NT
Pass	

The opening lead is a club and the opponents win four club tricks. On the fourth club trick East discards the nine of spades. At trick five West leads the three of spades. Dummy has discarded two small spades and has the ace and six of spades remaining. East has made a discard of the nine of spades, so the king of spades is probably with East. Moreover, South has eight tricks on top, if the hearts divide 3-3, there are already nine tricks.

There is really no reason to finesse in spades. After winning trick five with the ace of spades, do you think South should play three rounds of hearts to see whether or not the opponents' hearts break evenly and, if not, to concede one down?

This would be a very bad play. South should realize that if East or West holds the king of spades as well as four or more hearts, he will have difficulty in his discarding when South plays four rounds of diamonds before the hearts. On the fourth round of diamonds, dummy has the worthless six of spades to discard, but how about East or West who holds originally the king of spades together with four hearts?

In fact, South can cash the ace and queen of hearts before playing on the diamonds. On the fourth round of diamonds, i.e. at trick 11, the situation will be as follows:

(1)

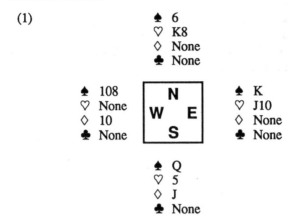

```
              ♠ 6
              ♡ K8
              ◊ None
              ♣ None

  ♠ 108                      ♠ K
  ♡ None       N             ♡ J10
  ◊ 10      W     E          ◊ None
  ♣ None       S             ♣ None

              ♠ Q
              ♡ 5
              ◊ J
              ♣ None
```

This is one of the most basic situations in the simple squeeze. Every player has three cards. South's queen of spades is a one-card menace against East's king of spades; North's king-eight of hearts is a two-card menace against East's jack-ten of hearts. South has a small card in the suit of this two-card menace, which can be led to North's master card.

South leads the jack of diamonds—the squeeze-card, North throws the six of spades, and East is squeezed in spades and hearts. If he discards the king of spades, South's queen of spades wins a trick, and North's king of hearts wins the last trick; if he discards a heart, North's king-eight of hearts win the last two tricks.

Observe that the above line of play does not abandon the chance of an even break in hearts. On the contrary, the play also takes this possibility into consideration and works equally well in this case.

It is easy to see that the four conditions of a squeeze described at the beginning of Chapter 1 are satisfied. Firstly, East has the only stoppers in spades and hearts. Secondly, there is a squeeze-card, namely the jack of diamonds in the South hand. Thirdly, at the time the squeeze-card is led, East's cards are all busy. Fourthly, the entries for the squeeze are appropriate: on the lead of the jack of diamonds, if East discards the king of spades, South has the lead and so can immediately cash the queen of spades; if East discards a heart, North has an entry in the heart suit itself to cash the newly established heart winner—the eight of hearts.

In diagram (1), if the East and West hands are interchanged, West will be subjected to the same squeeze. The situation in (1) is therefore an automatic simple squeeze. That is to say, the squeeze is equally effective against either opponent. The squeeze succeeds as long as the king of spades and the jack-ten of hearts are in one hand.

When the East and West hands are interchanged, the squeeze succeeds even if the queen of spades is in the North hand:

(2)

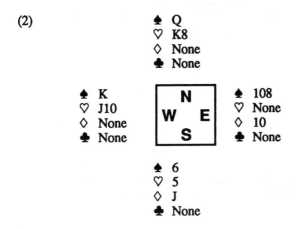

```
              ♠ Q
              ♡ K8
              ◊ None
              ♣ None
  ♠ K          ┌───────┐      ♠ 108
  ♡ J10        │   N   │      ♡ None
  ◊ None       │ W   E │      ◊ 10
  ♣ None       │   S   │      ♣ None
              └───────┘
              ♠ 6
              ♡ 5
              ◊ J
              ♣ None
```

This is the simplest form of the positional simple squeeze. South leads the jack of diamonds, West is squeezed. If he discards the king of spades, North's queen of spades becomes a winner; if he discards a heart, the king-eight of hearts win the last two tricks.

This positional squeeze is effective only against West.

The four conditions of a squeeze are all satisfied: West has the only stoppers in spades and hearts; South's jack of diamonds is the squeeze-card; all West's cards are busy; the two-card menace in the North hand has an entry card in the suit which can be used to cash the new winner set up by the forcing discard.

The following hand is an example.

♠ A95
♡ QJ62
◇ 1073
♣ 984

♠ K64
♡ K75
◇ AKQJ2
♣ AK

Against South's six no-trump contract West leads the queen of spades, which is won with the king. A small heart is played from South and dummy's jack goes to East's ace. A spade is returned, and West's ten forces out dummy's ace.

If the hearts break 3-3, there are twelve tricks. But suppose the hearts do not break evenly, then an immediate play of the king and queen of hearts would destroy every possibility of making the contract.

It is obvious that West has the jack of spades. If he also held four or more hearts originally then he is the opponent with the only stoppers in spades and hearts. South plays four rounds of diamonds as well as the king of hearts and the ace-king of clubs to arrive at the following end position:

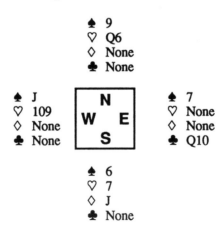

West is squeezed on the lead of the jack of diamonds. The situation is similar to that of (2).

The full deal is as follows:

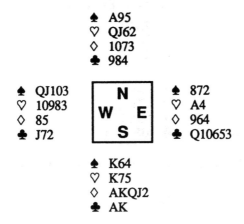

```
                    ♠  A95
                    ♡  QJ62
                    ◊  1073
                    ♣  984
    ♠  QJ103      ┌──────────┐    ♠  872
    ♡  10983      │    N     │    ♡  A4
    ◊  85         │ W      E │    ◊  964
    ♣  J72        │    S     │    ♣  Q10653
                  └──────────┘
                    ♠  K64
                    ♡  K75
                    ◊  AKQJ2
                    ♣  AK
```

In diagram (2) the two-card menace against West can be replaced by a split two-card menace to obtain another basic form of the positional simple squeeze:

*(3)

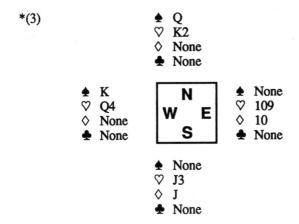

```
                    ♠  Q
                    ♡  K2
                    ◊  None
                    ♣  None
    ♠  K          ┌──────────┐    ♠  None
    ♡  Q4         │    N     │    ♡  109
    ◊  None       │ W      E │    ◊  10
    ♣  None       │    S     │    ♣  None
                  └──────────┘
                    ♠  None
                    ♡  J3
                    ◊  J
                    ♣  None
```

South leads the jack of diamonds. If West discards the king of spades, North's king of hearts and queen of spades win the last two tricks. If West discards the four of hearts, North lets go of the queen of spades. The three of hearts is led to the king, and the jack of hearts wins the last trick.

This is illustrated in the following hand.

East-West game; Dealer West

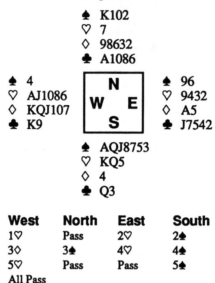

```
                ♠ K102
                ♡ 7
                ◊ 98632
                ♣ A1086
    ♠ 4                        ♠ 96
    ♡ AJ1086     N             ♡ 9432
    ◊ KQJ107   W   E           ◊ A5
    ♣ K9         S             ♣ J7542
                ♠ AQJ8753
                ♡ KQ5
                ◊ 4
                ♣ Q3
```

West	North	East	South
1♡	Pass	2♡	2♠
3◊	3♣	4♡	4♠
5♡	Pass	Pass	5♠
All Pass			

West leads the king of diamonds, East overtakes with the ace and returns the five, which South ruffs.

Two rounds of trumps are drawn and the king of hearts is conceded to West's ace. West leads another diamond, which South ruffs. The queen of hearts is cashed and South's last heart is led and ruffed in dummy. Another diamond is led and ruffed in the declarer's hand. Now a spade lead leaves this situation:

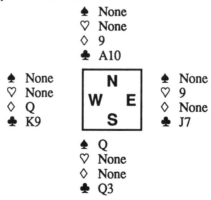

```
                ♠ None
                ♡ None
                ◊ 9
                ♣ A10
    ♠ None                     ♠ None
    ♡ None       N             ♡ 9
    ◊ Q        W   E           ◊ None
    ♣ K9         S             ♣ J7
                ♠ Q
                ♡ None
                ◊ None
                ♣ Q3
```

The lead of the queen of spades squeezes West in diamonds and clubs. The diamond discard sets up dummy's nine and a club discard enables North-South to win two tricks in clubs.

Another very important basic form of the simple squeeze can be obtained from the following hand.

♠ J63
♡ 964
◇ A9653
♣ Q4

♠ A
♡ AKQJ852
◇ K72
♣ AK

South	West	North	East
1♣[1]	Pass	1◇[2]	2♠
3♡	Pass	4♡	Pass
4NT	Pass	5◇	Pass
5NT	Pass	6♣	Pass
7♡	All Pass		

[1]Precision, 16+
[2]Negative

West leads the eight of spades to the three, nine and ace. South has twelve winners only, the thirteenth comes from a squeeze.

It seems likely that East has the king-queen of spades and may also hold three or more diamonds. In this case South can play six rounds of trumps together with the ace-king of clubs to leave this position:

*(4)

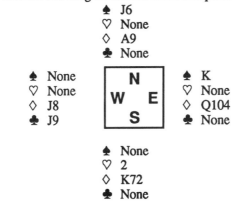

```
                ♠ J6
                ♡ None
                ◇ A9
                ♣ None
    ♠ None          N        ♠ K
    ♡ None      W       E    ♡ None
    ◇ J8            S        ◇ Q104
    ♣ J9                     ♣ None
                ♠ None
                ♡ 2
                ◇ K72
                ♣ None
```

25

South has three winners out of the remaining four cards. The two of hearts is the squeeze-card. The jack of spades is a one-card menace against East's king of spades. The North-South diamond combination is a split three-card menace against East with the three-card part in the same hand as the squeeze-card. South leads the two of hearts, throwing North's lets go the idle card—the six of spades, and East is squeezed in spades and diamonds. If East discards the king of spades, North's jack of spades becomes a winner, the ace of diamonds being the entry to the North hand to cash it. If East discards a diamond, North-South win three tricks in diamonds.

This ending is the second basic form of the automatic simple squeeze. The squeeze is equally effective if the East-West hands are interchanged.

In this situation, it is clear that the four conditions of a simple squeeze are satisfied: East has the only stoppers in spades and diamonds; South has a squeeze-card—the two of hearts; all East's cards are busy; both North and South have necessary entries after the squeeze-card is played.

We have described four basic simple-squeeze positions. They are the most fundamental and most frequently encountered squeeze situations in practice. The situations in (1) and (4) are automatic, effective against either opponent, while those in (2) and (3) are positional, effective only against the opponent to the left of the squeeze-card.

We now summarise in brief how a squeeze can be planned and executed in play.

In playing a hand, if various methods have been examined and none is satisfactory, the possibility of a squeeze can be taken into consideration. According to the four conditions that must be satisfied by a squeeze, the problem is approached as follows:

Firstly, inspect carefully whether there are two suits in which one opponent has the only winners or stoppers.

Secondly, if this is the case (in actual play a declarer often assumes that the only stoppers of certain suits are held by a certain opponent), count the number of busy cards in that opponent's hand. Then, by some means or other, try to remove from that opponent's hand all idle cards (for example, let the opponents win some tricks that are certain to lose), until the declarer's cards are reduced to the same number as the opponent's busy cards.

Thirdly, the menaces must be in their proper places to ensure the effectiveness of the squeeze.

Finally, lead the squeeze-card and cash the new winner produced by the opponent's discard.

In a word, we must play the hand to an end position which is exactly the same as one of the familiar basic squeeze situations. It is, therefore, quite necessary to memorise a few of the basic squeeze diagrams. This will certainly help in the recognition of squeeze positions.

2.2 The Vienna Coup and the menace transfer

It may happen that, in order to unblock a suit, the declarer should first play the master card of that suit, thus promoting an opponent's card to the highest rank, only to effect a squeeze against him at a later trick. This play of the master card of a suit is called the Vienna Coup.

South plays three no-trumps in the following hand.

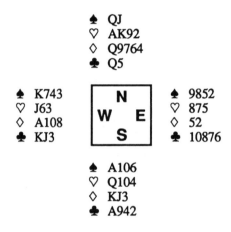

```
              ♠ QJ
              ♡ AK92
              ◊ Q9764
              ♣ Q5

  ♠ K743      ┌─────────┐    ♠ 9852
  ♡ J63       │   N     │    ♡ 875
  ◊ A108      │ W     E │    ◊ 52
  ♣ KJ3       │   S     │    ♣ 10876
              └─────────┘
              ♠ A106
              ♡ Q104
              ◊ KJ3
              ♣ A942
```

West leads the three of spades, dummy's jack winning. A small diamond is led to the king and ace. At trick three West leads the three of hearts, which is taken by South's ten.

The declarer has eleven tricks since the diamonds break 3-2. A twelfth trick is possible if West holds both black kings.

However, before cashing all the red winners the declarer should play the ace of clubs (the Vienna Coup). This is the three-card ending:

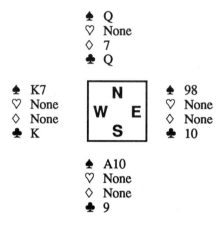

On the lead of dummy's last diamond, South discards the nine of clubs, and West is subjected to a simple automatic squeeze. The situation is the same as in diagram (1).

If the ace of clubs had not been cashed earlier in the play, the situation would have been:

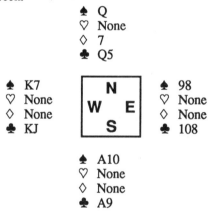

On the lead of the seven of diamonds, South would be squeezed before West. In fact, the Vienna Coup turns a positional squeeze into an automatic squeeze.

A play similar to the Vienna Coup is the "menace transfer". Before effecting a squeeze, the declarer plans to kill a high card of a certain opponent, say West's king of hearts. Suppose South leads the queen of hearts, West has to cover with the king, and North's ace wins. Now the ten of hearts in the South or North hand becomes a single menace against East's knave. Originally the menaced opponent is West, but now it is East who is threatened in the heart suit. If there is sufficient reason to believe that the king of hearts is with West, this is a useful technique.

Of course, the declarer plays on the assumption that East has the jack of hearts, and the position of the ten of hearts must be in conformity with the conditions of the subsequent simple squeeze against East.

This is illustrated in the following hand.

Love all; Dealer West

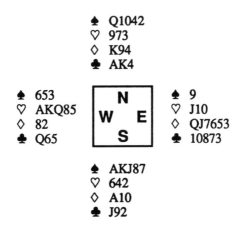

♠ Q1042
♡ 973
◇ K94
♣ AK4

♠ 653   ♠ 9
♡ AKQ85 ♡ J10
◇ 82   ◇ QJ7653
♣ Q65   ♣ 10873

♠ AKJ87
♡ 642
◇ A10
♣ J92

West opens one heart and South eventually becomes declarer in four spades.

West wins the first three tricks with the king, ace and queen of hearts, East discarding the seven of diamonds on the third round. At trick four, West leads the eight of diamonds and East's jack is taken by South's ace. The ten, queen and ace of trumps win the next three tricks.

It seems that West has no high cards in diamond, so he must hold the queen of clubs to justify his opening bid. The jack of clubs is therefore led at trick eight. When this is covered by West's queen, North plays the king. The declarer hopes that the ten of clubs is in the East hand so that the nine of clubs can be used as a one-card menace against East. The ace of clubs is also cashed (Vienna Coup) and another trump lead leaves this ending:

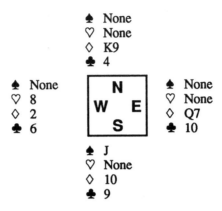

```
            ♠ None
            ♡ None
            ◊ K9
            ♣ 4
♠ None              ♠ None
♡ 8      N         ♡ None
◊ 2   W     E      ◊ Q7
♣ 6      S         ♣ 10
            ♠ J
            ♡ None
            ◊ 10
            ♣ 9
```

The lead of the jack of spades squeezes East in diamonds and clubs. The situation is again the same as in diagram (1).

The lead of the jack of clubs forces West to cover with the queen. This is the menace-transfer play. The jack of clubs as a menace card against West's queen disappears, and the nine of clubs as a new menace card against East's ten comes into existence.

2.3 Simple squeezes without "all-but-one"

Sometimes a squeeze can involve a forcing discard combined with a trick-establishing play. On the lead of the declarer's squeeze-card, an opponent is forced to discard one of his winners. The declarer then concedes a trick in a suit to set up a card in that suit as a new winner. In this case the declarer cannot win all but one of the remaining tricks when the squeeze begins.

(5)

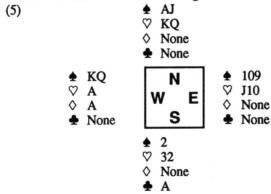

```
                ♠ AJ
                ♡ KQ
                ◊ None
                ♣ None
♠ KQ                    ♠ 109
♡ A        N           ♡ J10
◊ A     W     E        ◊ None
♣ None     S           ♣ None
                ♠ 2
                ♡ 32
                ◊ None
                ♣ A
```

On the lead of the ace of clubs, West has to discard his diamond winner, and North lets go of the jack of spades. A heart is led at the next trick, establishing a heart winner in the North hand. This squeeze situation is obviously positional.

The following hand is played by South in a contract of three no-trumps.

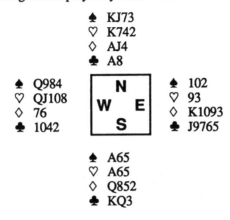

```
                    ♠  KJ73
                    ♡  K742
                    ◊  AJ4
                    ♣  A8
    ♠  Q984        ┌─────────┐      ♠  102
    ♡  QJ108       │    N    │      ♡  93
    ◊  76          │  W   E  │      ◊  K1093
    ♣  1042        │    S    │      ♣  J9765
                   └─────────┘
                    ♠  A65
                    ♡  A65
                    ◊  Q852
                    ♣  KQ3
```

West leads the queen of hearts, won by South's ace. A diamond is led to dummy's jack and East's king. East returns the nine of hearts, dummy's king winning. The ace and king of clubs are cashed. At trick six, a spade is led from South. When West plays low, North finesses the jack, which holds. The declarer then cashes the ace of spades, the ace and queen of diamonds, and the queen of clubs. On the lead of the queen of clubs, West is squeezed:

(6)

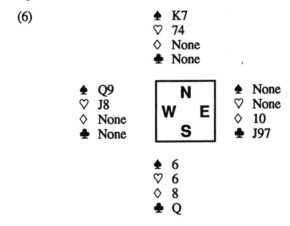

```
                    ♠  K7
                    ♡  74
                    ◊  None
                    ♣  None
    ♠  Q9          ┌─────────┐      ♠  None
    ♡  J8          │    N    │      ♡  None
    ◊  None        │  W   E  │      ◊  10
    ♣  None        │    S    │      ♣  J97
                   └─────────┘
                    ♠  6
                    ♡  6
                    ◊  8
                    ♣  Q
```

If West discards a spade, North wins two spade tricks. If West discards a heart, North lets go of the seven of spades. South then leads the six of hearts, setting up a heart winner in the North hand. South makes three no-trumps with two overtricks.

In both diagrams (5) and (6), North's heart suit is an extended one-card menace against West. Once West discards the ace of diamonds in (5) or a heart in (6), a small heart will be led from the South hand, and a heart winner will be established in the North hand.

The extended one-card menace in the North hand in either (5) or (6) can be transferred to the South hand without destroying the squeeze. This enables two more positional situations to exist:

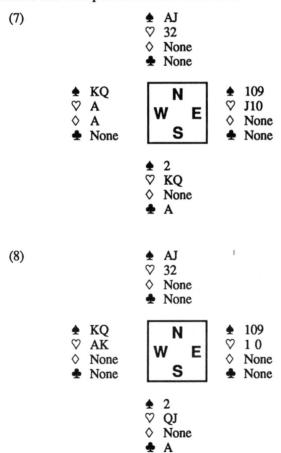

(7)

```
              ♠ AJ
              ♡ 32
              ◊ None
              ♣ None

♠ KQ        ┌─────────┐        ♠ 109
♡ A         │    N    │        ♡ J10
◊ A         │  W   E  │        ◊ None
♣ None      │    S    │        ♣ None
            └─────────┘
              ♠ 2
              ♡ KQ
              ◊ None
              ♣ A
```

(8)

```
              ♠ AJ
              ♡ 32
              ◊ None
              ♣ None

♠ KQ        ┌─────────┐        ♠ 109
♡ AK        │    N    │        ♡ 1 0
◊ None      │  W   E  │        ◊ None
♣ None      │    S    │        ♣ None
            └─────────┘
              ♠ 2
              ♡ QJ
              ◊ None
              ♣ A
```

It should be noted that, in these situations, North must have two small hearts, otherwise South cannot cash a heart winner after it has become established.

An automatic-squeeze positioncan be obtained by introducing a split three-card menace:

(9)

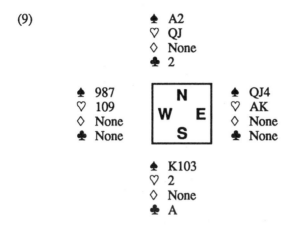

South plays the ace of clubs and East is squeezed.
A similar situation is this:

(10)

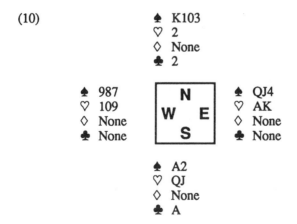

Like the situation in diagram (9), this is also an automatic-squeeze position.

A squeeze can also be a combination of a forcing discard and a throw-in play. An opponent is forced to discard a winner and is then thrown in to make a lead into a major tenace.

(11)

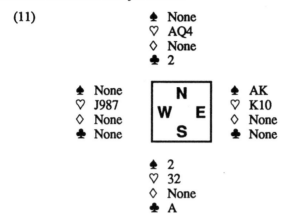

	♠ None	
	♡ AQ4	
	◊ None	
	♣ 2	

♠ None		♠ AK
♡ J987		♡ K10
◊ None		◊ None
♣ None		♣ None

	♠ 2	
	♡ 32	
	◊ None	
	♣ A	

The lead of the ace of clubs forces East to discard a spade winner. The two of spades is then led, and East is obliged to lead a heart into North's ace-queen.

North-South game; Dealer West

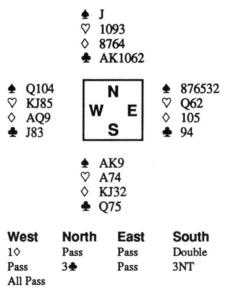

	♠ J	
	♡ 1093	
	◊ 8764	
	♣ AK1062	

♠ Q104		♠ 876532
♡ KJ85		♡ Q62
◊ AQ9		◊ 105
♣ J83		♣ 94

	♠ AK9	
	♡ A74	
	◊ KJ32	
	♣ Q75	

West	North	East	South
1◊	Pass	Pass	Double
Pass	3♣	Pass	3NT
All Pass			

34

Hearts are led and continued, South winning the third round. The declarer plays on clubs and, at trick eight, the situation is as follows:

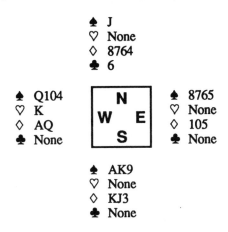

♠ J
♡ None
♢ 8764
♣ 6

♠ Q104   ♠ 8765
♡ K   ♡ None
♢ AQ   ♢ 105
♣ None   ♣ None

♠ AK9
♡ None
♢ KJ3
♣ None

All the unseen high cards are in the West hand. When the six of clubs is led from dummy, South discards the three of diamonds and West is squeezed. If he discards a spade, South can win three tricks in spades. If he discards the heart winner, South plays the ace, king and nine of spades and can win another trick with the king of diamonds. If West discards the queen of diamonds, North leads a diamond. West can take his two winners, but South wins the last three tricks.

This example shows that when a squeeze begins, the opponent squeezed may have two or more winners. To put it another way, the squeezing side may have two or more losers. It also shows that the opponent squeezed may have to lead away from a major tenace when he is put on lead after the forcing discard.

2.4 The criss-cross squeeze

There remains to be described one important basic form of the simple squeeze:

(12)
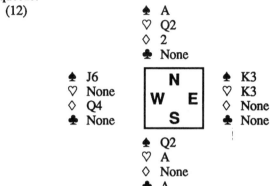

The ace of clubs is the squeeze-card. The spade suit and the heart suit are two split two-card menaces against East.

South leads the ace of clubs, North discards the two of diamonds, and East is squeezed in spades and hearts. If East discards the three of spades, South wins the ace of spades, the ace of hearts and the queen of spades in turn. If East discards the three of hearts, South plays the ace of hearts, and North's ace of spades and queen of hearts win the last two tricks.

The squeeze is automatic: if the East and West hands are interchanged, West will be squeezed. This basic position, called a "criss-cross" squeeze, is unique in the simple squeeze.

The next hand is an example.

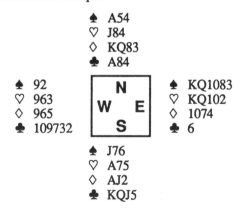

The contract is three no-trumps by South. West leads the nine of spades, dummy plays low, and East's queen wins. East leads the king of hearts, which is allowed to win. At trick three, East switches to a diamond. It is rather clear that East holds protection in both major suits. By running both minor suits, the declarer can arrive at the following ending:

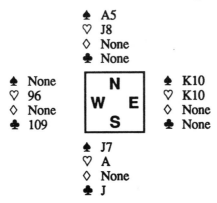

```
            ♠ A5
            ♡ J8
            ◇ None
            ♣ None
♠ None    ┌─────────┐   ♠ K10
♡ 96      │    N    │   ♡ K10
◇ None    │ W     E │   ◇ None
♣ 109     │    S    │   ♣ None
          └─────────┘
            ♠ J7
            ♡ A
            ◇ None
            ♣ J
```

South leads the jack of clubs, on which North discards the five of spades, and East is squeezed in spades and hearts. The declarer makes eleven tricks through a criss-cross squeeze.

2.5 The jettison simple squeeze and the nosittej simple squeeze

The basic end position for a jettison simple squeeze can be derived from the following hand.

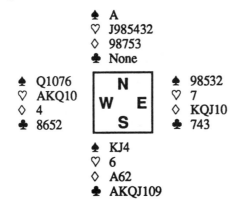

```
            ♠ A
            ♡ J985432
            ◇ 98753
            ♣ None
♠ Q1076   ┌─────────┐   ♠ 98532
♡ AKQ10   │    N    │   ♡ 7
◇ 4       │ W     E │   ◇ KQJ10
♣ 8652    │    S    │   ♣ 743
          └─────────┘
            ♠ KJ4
            ♡ 6
            ◇ A62
            ♣ AKQJ109
```

The contract is three no-trumps by South. West wins the first two tricks with the king and queen of hearts, East discards the two of spades and South the four of spades.

West then leads the four of diamonds and East wins the third and fourth tricks with the ten and king of diamonds. At trick five, East leads another diamond to the declarer's ace. The declarer plays five rounds of clubs and the situation at trick 11 is:

(13)

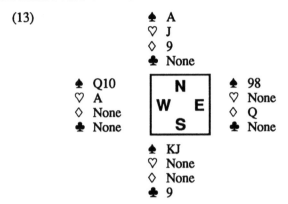

South leads the nine of clubs and West is squeezed. If West discards the ace of hearts, North lets go of the nine of diamonds, and North's ace of spades and jack of hearts win the last two tricks. If West discards a spade, North jettisons the ace of spades, and South's king-jack of spades make two tricks. This positional simple squeeze is called a jettison squeeze. Now, let us swap North's ace and South's king of spades to obtain the following situation:

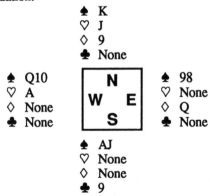

On the lead of the nine of clubs, West is squeezed. If he discards a spade, South's ace and jack of spades win two tricks. If he discards the ace of hearts, North's king of spades and jack of hearts win two tricks.

This squeeze is the natural reverse of the jettison squeeze. We may call it a *nosittej squeeze*. Moreover, this nosittej squeeze is automatic: if the East and West hands are interchanged, East will be squeezed:

(14)

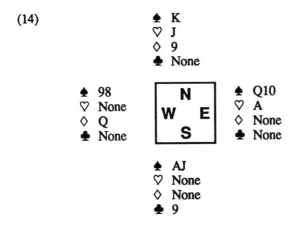

```
                    ♠  K
                    ♡  J
                    ◇  9
                    ♣  None

    ♠  98        ┌─────────┐      ♠  Q10
    ♡  None      │    N    │      ♡  A
    ◇  Q         │  W   E  │      ◇  None
    ♣  None      │    S    │      ♣  None
                 └─────────┘
                    ♠  AJ
                    ♡  None
                    ◇  None
                    ♣  9
```

On the lead of the nine of clubs, North throws the nine of diamonds and East is nosittej-squeezed: the discard of the ace of hearts makes good North's king of spades and jack of hearts, and a spade discard permits South to score the ace and jack of spades.#

* The situations in diagrams (13) and (14) were first published in *The British Bridge World*, December 1956.

Chapter 3

Double Squeezes

3.1 The two fundamental forms

A double squeeze is a combination of two simple squeezes, one against each opponent. Ordinarily it involves three suits. One opponent is squeezed in two suits, the other opponent is also squeezed in two suits. In one suit both opponents have stoppers; the other two suits are guarded separately by the two opponents.

Let us study this hand:

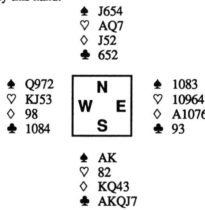

```
              ♠  J654
              ♡  AQ7
              ◊  J52
              ♣  652

  ♠  Q972    ┌─────────┐    ♠  1083
  ♡  KJ53    │   N     │    ♡  10964
  ◊  98      │ W   E   │    ◊  A1076
  ♣  1084    │   S     │    ♣  93
             └─────────┘
              ♠  AK
              ♡  82
              ◊  KQ43
              ♣  AKQJ7
```

The contract is six clubs by South. West leads the nine of diamonds, which is won with South's queen. After three rounds of trumps, the declarer leads a small diamond to dummy's jack and East's ace. The declarer wins the diamond return, disclosing that East has the fourth-round diamond guard. The declarer cashes the ace and king of spades, but the queen does not drop. A finesse in hearts is then taken, which succeeds. A spade is led and ruffed, the queen still does not appear.

The declarer has a losing diamond in the South hand. If the queen of spades is in the East hand, a simple squeeze against East in spades and diamonds cannot work, since there is no two-card menace and hence no necessary entry.

How about a simple squeeze against East in hearts and diamonds? The chances are against it: it would require East to hold six or more hearts originally. In this case dummy's seven of hearts can be used as a menace card against East.

Now let us see what will happen if the queen of spades is in the West hand. Dummy's jack of spades becomes a one-card menace against West's queen of spades, and this menace card lies behind West. Besides, West has the duty to guard the heart suit. The four of diamonds in the South hand is a one-card menace against East's ten of diamonds, and this menace card lies behind East. East also has the duty of protecting hearts. Therefore, it is possible to form a double squeeze against both opponents.

Ten tricks have been played. The situation now is:

(15)

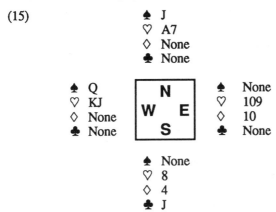

```
                    ♠  J
                    ♡  A7
                    ◇  None
                    ♣  None

    ♠  Q          ┌───────────┐        ♠  None
    ♡  KJ         │     N     │        ♡  109
    ◇  None       │  W     E  │        ◇  10
    ♣  None       │     S     │        ♣  None
                  └───────────┘
                    ♠  None
                    ♡  8
                    ◇  4
                    ♣  J
```

South leads the jack of clubs. West, in order to retain the queen of spades, is forced to part with a heart. Now he can no longer guard the heart suit. In fact, if we regard the West and East hands separately, West is simple-squeezed in spades and hearts on the lead of the jack of clubs. After West discards a heart, North's jack of spades, which has accomplished its task of threatening West, becomes worthless, and can be discarded.

East, who now alone holds stoppers in both hearts and diamonds, is squeezed likewise. The diamond discard sets up South's four of diamonds, a heart discard enables the declarer to win two tricks in that suit.

The position in (15) is the commonest basic double-squeeze position. These are the requirements: South has a squeeze-card, namely the jack of clubs, and a one-card menace against East. North has a one-card menace against West and a two-card double menace against both opponents, including a master card. Besides, South has a small card in the double-menace suit. This is necessary to ensure an entry to the North hand.

We have seen that each of the two one-card menaces is situated at the left of the opponent threatened, and the two-card double menace is in the hand opposite the squeeze-card. If we decompose this double squeeze into two simple squeezes, each one satisfies the four conditions of a simple squeeze which we have analysed in Section 1.1. That is to say, each opponent guards two suits, one of which is guarded by both opponents; there is a squeeze-card in the South hand; the cards of both opponents are busy; and North-South have sufficient entries after the squeeze-card is led.

In diagram (15), when South leads the squeeze-card, West and East are squeezed at the same trick. It is called a *simultaneous* double squeeze. If the situation is such that one opponent is squeezed first, while his partner is squeezed at a later trick, it is called a *non-simultaneous* double squeeze.

Besides, in the position shown in (15), North's cards are all busy. The squeeze is positional; it fails if the East-West hands are interchanged.

Actually, the situation in (15) is equivalent to a combination of (2) and (1). Diagram (2) is a positional simple squeeze against West, and diagram (1) is an automatic simple squeeze against East.

A second basic double-squeeze position can be obtained from the following hand.

♠ AJ2
♡ KQ53
◇ QJ9
♣ K84

```
┌─────────┐
│    N    │
│ W     E │
│    S    │
└─────────┘
```

♠ KQ864
♡ A62
◇ A4
♣ A76

The contract is six spades by South. West leads the jack of hearts, which is won with dummy's queen. After three rounds of trumps, the queen of diamonds is led from dummy. East and South play low, and the queen holds. North-South have a chance of making thirteen tricks.

The ace of diamonds is cashed. Dummy's jack of diamonds is now a one-card menace against East's king of diamonds. The king and ace of hearts are played, East discarding a diamond on the ace of hearts. Dummy's five of hearts becomes a one-card menace against West.

South plays another spade, North discards a club, and the position is:

(16)

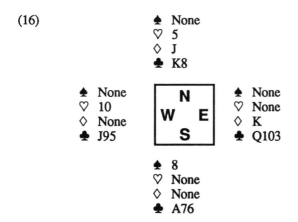

	♠ None
	♡ 5
	◊ J
	♣ K8

♠ None	♠ None
♡ 10	♡ None
◊ None	◊ K
♣ J95	♣ Q103

	♠ 8
	♡ None
	◊ None
	♣ A76

South leads the eight of spades, and West is squeezed. If West discards the ten of hearts, North's five of hearts becomes a winner. If West discards a club, North lets go the now useless five of hearts, and East is squeezed in diamonds and clubs.

This is another important basic form of the double squeeze. It is again a simultaneous squeeze, West and East are squeezed at the same trick. The requirements are as follows: South has a squeeze-card; North has two one-card menaces, one against each opponent; there is a split three-card double menace with the three-card part in the same hand as the squeeze-card.

Although the squeeze works equally well if the West and East hands are interchanged, the declarer must make sure which one of North's two one-card menaces is against West. Here the five of hearts is a single menace against West, while the jack of diamonds is against East. If the declarer mistakes one single menace for the other, he cannot make the correct discard in the North hand after West discards a club. We therefore do not identify the situation with an automatic squeeze.

The situation in (16) is equivalent to the combination of two simple squeezes similar to the one in diagram (4). On the lead of the squeeze-card, both West and East are squeezed in a manner which is practically the same as in (4), except that the split three-card menace in (16) is not a single menace against one certain opponent. It is a split three-card double menace against both opponents.

The full deal is as follows:

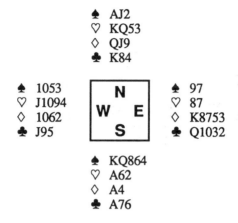

```
            ♠ AJ2
            ♡ KQ53
            ◇ QJ9
            ♣ K84
♠ 1053          N          ♠ 97
♡ J1094                    ♡ 87
◇ 1062     W       E       ◇ K8753
♣ J95          S           ♣ Q1032
            ♠ KQ864
            ♡ A62
            ◇ A4
            ♣ A76
```

3.2 Non-simultaneous double squeezes

Let us examine the following hand:

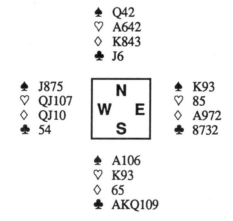

```
            ♠ Q42
            ♡ A642
            ◇ K843
            ♣ J6
♠ J875          N          ♠ K93
♡ QJ107                    ♡ 85
◇ QJ10     W       E       ◇ A972
♣ 54           S           ♣ 8732
            ♠ A106
            ♡ K93
            ◇ 65
            ♣ AKQ109
```

South is declarer at three no-trumps. West takes the first three tricks with the queen, jack and ten of diamonds, South discarding the six of spades. At trick four, West leads the ten of hearts which is allowed to win. The jack of hearts is led at trick five, South's king winning.

South plays four rounds of clubs, leaving this position at trick ten:

(17)

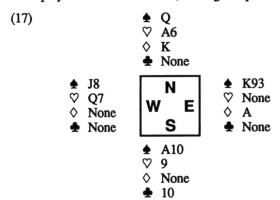

```
              ♠ Q
              ♡ A6
              ◊ K
              ♣ None
♠ J8        ┌─────────┐      ♠ K93
♡ Q7        │    N    │      ♡ None
◊ None      │  W   E  │      ◊ A
♣ None      │    S    │      ♣ None
            └─────────┘
              ♠ A10
              ♡ 9
              ◊ None
              ♣ 10
```

The lead of the ten of clubs squeezes West in spades and hearts. West has to part with a spade. North lets go of the six of hearts, East the three of spades. At the next trick the nine of hearts is led to the ace, and East is squeezed in spades and diamonds.

This double squeeze is positional. If the East and West hands are interchanged, West would have an idle card to discard on the lead of the ten of clubs, and North would be squeezed before East.

This is a non-simultaneous double squeeze. West is squeezed first, and East is squeezed at the next trick.

In diagram (17), if South has an additional master card in the double, menace suit, the situation becomes:

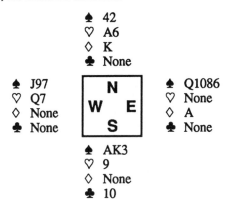

```
              ♠ 42
              ♡ A6
              ◊ K
              ♣ None
♠ J97       ┌─────────┐      ♠ Q1086
♡ Q7        │    N    │      ♡ None
◊ None      │  W   E  │      ◊ A
♣ None      │    S    │      ♣ None
            └─────────┘
              ♠ AK3
              ♡ 9
              ◊ None
              ♣ 10
```

South plays the ten of clubs, and, just as in the case of diagram (17), West is squeezed first. In order to preserve the hearts, West is forced to discard a spade. North also discards a spade. At the next trick North's ace of hearts squeezes East in spades and diamonds.

Unlike the situation in (17), here North has an idle card to discard when the ten of clubs is led. This double-squeeze situation is therefore an automatic double squeeze. It is equally effective if the West and East hands are interchanged:

(18)

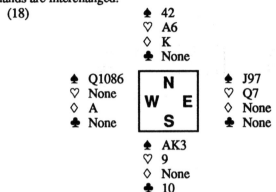

```
              ♠  42
              ♡  A6
              ◊  K
              ♣  None

♠  Q1086       N        ♠  J97
♡  None    W       E    ♡  Q7
◊  A                    ◊  None
♣  None        S        ♣  None

              ♠  AK3
              ♡  9
              ◊  None
              ♣  10
```

South leads the ten of clubs, North discards a spade, and East is squeezed first. If he discards a heart, North's ace-six of hearts can win two tricks. If he discards a spade, at the next trick the ace of hearts squeezes West in spades and diamonds.

The situation in (18) is a non-simultaneous automatic double squeeze. The opponent who guards hearts is squeezed first since he has no idle card in his hand. The other opponent is squeezed at the next trick.

Here is an example.

North-South game; Dealer East

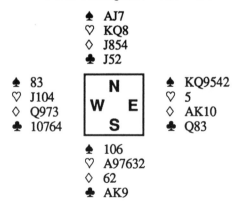

```
              ♠  AJ7
              ♡  KQ8
              ◊  J854
              ♣  J52

♠  83          N        ♠  KQ9542
♡  J104    W       E    ♡  5
◊  Q973                 ◊  AK10
♣  10764       S        ♣  Q83

              ♠  106
              ♡  A97632
              ◊  62
              ♣  AK9
```

West leads the eight of spades, North plays low, and East's queen wins. East plays three rounds of diamonds, South ruffing the third round. South plays four rounds of trumps and arrives at this ending:

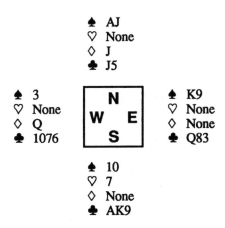

This is the same non-simultaneous automatic double squeeze as in (18). The lead of the seven of hearts begins the squeeze against East who must discard a club. At the next trick the ace of spades squeezes West in diamonds and clubs.

The situations in diagrams (15) to (18) are the four most important basic double-squeeze endings. They must be learned by heart.

3.3 A simultaneous automatic double squeeze

The situations in diagrams (15) and (16) are simultaneous positional double squeezes. Diagrams (17) and (18) are non-simultaneous double, squeeze situations, the former is positional and the latter automatic. The following hand contains a simultaneous automatic double squeeze.

♠ Q104
♡ A104
◇ AK104
♣ 1084

♠ 9763
♡ J96
◇ 9
♣ AQJ93

North opens the bidding with one diamond, and South bids one no-trump, which ends the auction.

West leads the two of spades, dummy plays low, and East's ace wins. East returns the five of spades to West's king. West leads the eight of hearts to the four and queen. At trick four East leads the two of clubs, South plays the queen and West wins. West leads another heart, dummy plays the ace.

The opponents have won four tricks. North-South have eight top-card winners. The declarer cashes dummy's queen of spades, East discarding a diamond. South then plays four rounds of clubs. Assuming the king of hearts is with East, on the fourth round of clubs the situation is:

(19)

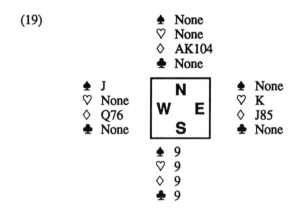

♠ None
♡ None
◇ AK104
♣ None

♠ J
♡ None
◇ Q76
♣ None

♠ None
♡ K
◇ J85
♣ None

♠ 9
♡ 9
◇ 9
♣ 9

South leads the nine of clubs—the squeeze-card. North discards the four of diamonds and both opponents are squeezed simultaneously. If West discards the jack of spades, or East discards the king of hearts, the nine of spades or the nine of hearts gains a trick. If both opponents discard in diamonds, North's ace-king-ten of diamonds win the last three tricks.

The basic situation in (19) is an automatic simultaneous double squeeze. This situation is rarely met in play, so it is not so important as the situations in diagrams (15) to (18).

3.4 Variations

The following is the simultaneous double-squeeze position shown in (16):

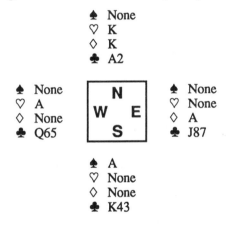

```
              ♠ None
              ♡ K
              ◊ K
              ♣ A2

  ♠ None                    ♠ None
  ♡ A      ┌─────────┐      ♡ None
  ◊ None   │ N       │      ◊ A
  ♣ Q65    │ W     E │      ♣ J87
           │    S    │
           └─────────┘
              ♠ A
              ♡ None
              ◊ None
              ♣ K43
```

At no-trumps, or with spades as trumps, the lead of the ace of spades squeezes West and East simultaneously.

In this situation it can be seen that the squeeze fails if the one-card menace against East is replaced by a longer menace. The one-card menace against West is not subject to this restriction, i.e. it may be replaced by a longer menace:

(20)

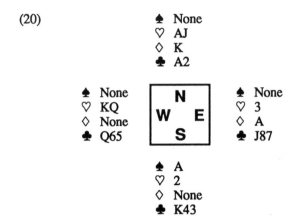

♠ None
♡ AJ
◇ K
♣ A2

♠ None ♠ None
♡ KQ ♡ 3
◇ None ◇ A
♣ Q65 ♣ J87

♠ A
♡ 2
◇ None
♣ K43

On the lead of the ace of spades, West, who is squeezed first, must discard a club. North throws the jack of hearts and, at the next trick, the ace of hearts squeezes East in the minors.

If the ace of hearts is played at an earlier stage, the position is reduced to the original one; if the ace of clubs is played at an earlier stage, the position is reduced to an inverted double squeeze:

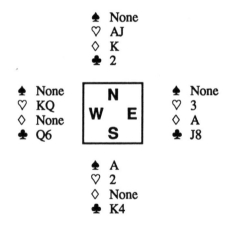

♠ None
♡ AJ
◇ K
♣ 2

♠ None ♠ None
♡ KQ ♡ 3
◇ None ◇ A
♣ Q6 ♣ J8

♠ A
♡ 2
◇ None
♣ K4

This is the non-simultaneous positional double squeeze of diagram (17). The lead of the ace of spades squeezes West, who must discard a club. North throws the jack of hearts. The ace of hearts is then played, squeezing East in diamonds and clubs.

However, in diagram (20), if South does not hold a card in the suit of the two-card menace against West, the fifth card being in the suit of the double menace, a new situation arises:

(21)

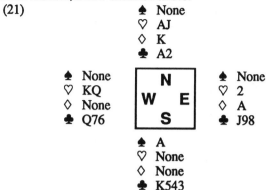

```
            ♠ None
            ♡ AJ
            ◇ K
            ♣ A2

♠ None                    ♠ None
♡ KQ        N             ♡ 2
◇ None    W   E           ◇ A
♣ Q76       S             ♣ J98

            ♠ A
            ♡ None
            ◇ None
            ♣ K543
```

On the lead of the ace of spades, West is squeezed and must discard a club. North throws the jack of hearts, East the two of hearts. A club is led to the ace, and the ace of hearts is played, squeezing East in simple-automatic fashion.

Here the ace of hearts is still allowed to be played at an earlier stage to leave a simultaneous-squeeze position. But it often happens that in the actual play a declarer has no opportunity to do the reduction. When this is the case the situation shown in diagram (21) must be brought about in order to effect the squeeze.

This is well illustrated in the following hand.

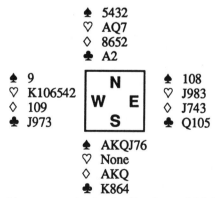

```
            ♠ 5432
            ♡ AQ7
            ◇ 8652
            ♣ A2

♠ 9                       ♠ 108
♡ K106542   N             ♡ J983
◇ 109     W   E           ◇ J743
♣ J973      S             ♣ Q105

            ♠ AKQJ76
            ♡ None
            ◇ AKQ
            ♣ K864
```

The contract is seven no-trumps by South, to which West leads the ten of diamonds. Since the ace of clubs is the only entry to dummy, there is no chance for the declarer to cash the ace of hearts before the double squeeze operates.

But, as West holds the king of hearts, the ace-queen of hearts serves as a two-card menace against him and the squeeze still works. The only distinction is that the situation here is non-simultaneous rather than simultaneous.

The end position is:

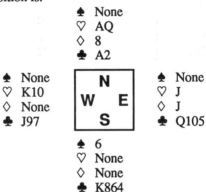

```
             ♠ None
             ♡ AQ
             ◊ 8
             ♣ A2
♠ None      ┌─────────┐   ♠ None
♡ K10       │   N     │   ♡ J
◊ None      │ W     E │   ◊ J
♣ J97       │   S     │   ♣ Q105
            └─────────┘
             ♠ 6
             ♡ None
             ◊ None
             ♣ K864
```

The situation is the same as in diagram (21).

The importance of this double-squeeze situation lies in the fact that the one-card menace against East may be in the same hand as the squeeze-card:[*]

(22)

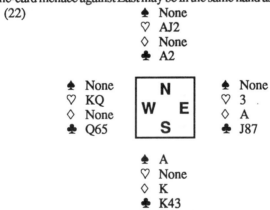

```
             ♠ None
             ♡ AJ2
             ◊ None
             ♣ A2
♠ None      ┌─────────┐   ♠ None
♡ KQ        │   N     │   ♡ 3
◊ None      │ W     E │   ◊ A
♣ Q65       │   S     │   ♣ J87
            └─────────┘
             ♠ A
             ♡ None
             ◊ K
             ♣ K43
```

Here the ace of hearts cannot be cashed earlier in play.

Unfortunately, this situation is inflexible and no variation is possible.

---

[*] This basic situation was first published in *Bridge Magazine*, September 1952, except that each of the two single menaces have been increased in length.

The following hand was played by me (South) many years ago.

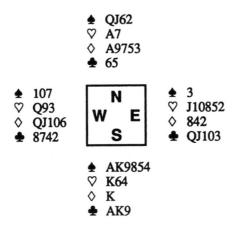

The final contract was seven no-trumps, and West led the queen of diamonds. When the dummy went down I regretted that I had not bid the hand to seven spades. Nevertheless, the contract was made by playing to the following end position:

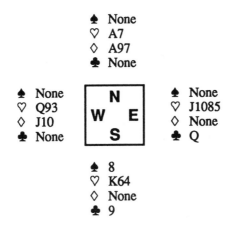

And this is exactly the same situation as in diagram (22). The eight of spades is the squeeze-card which begins the squeeze against West.

North's ace-nine of diamonds is a two-card menace against West, and South's nine of clubs is a one-card menace against East.

It should be noted that the ace of diamonds should not be cashed in the middle game, otherwise the declarer has to play for a simple squeeze which will certainly fail in this case.

3.5 Squeezing each opponent with his partner's menace suit

Sometimes in a double-squeeze situation there is no isolated squeeze-card, each opponent being squeezed by the lead of a card in his partner's menace suit. The following is a well-known basic situation of this type.

(23)

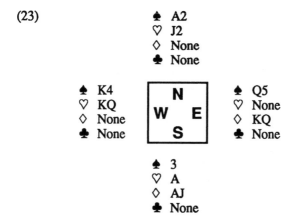

```
              ♠  A2
              ♡  J2
              ◇  None
              ♣  None

  ♠  K4      ┌─────────┐     ♠  Q5
  ♡  KQ      │    N    │     ♡  None
  ◇  None    │  W   E  │     ◇  KQ
  ♣  None    │    S    │     ♣  None
              └─────────┘
              ♠  3
              ♡  A
              ◇  AJ
              ♣  None
```

The spades in the North-South hands constitute a two-card double menace against both opponents, the heart suit is a split two-card menace against West, and the diamond suit is a two-card menace against East.

This is a non-simultaneous positional double squeeze and either opponent may be squeezed first. If the ace of hearts is led first, East is squeezed and has to discard a spade. At the next trick the ace of diamonds squeezes West in spades and hearts. If the ace of diamonds is led first, West is squeezed and has to discard a spade, while North lets go of a heart. At the next trick the ace of hearts squeezes East in spades and diamonds.

By introducing a split three-card double menace, I found two more basic situations of the type of squeeze in which each opponent is squeezed by the lead of a winner in his partner's menace suit. The first one is this:[*]

(24)

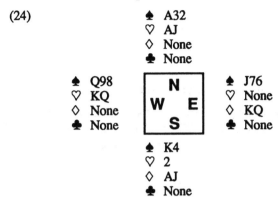

```
                    ♠  A32
                    ♡  AJ
                    ◊  None
                    ♣  None
     ♠  Q98         N          ♠  J76
     ♡  KQ                     ♡  None
     ◊  None     W     E       ◊  KQ
     ♣  None        S          ♣  None
                    ♠  K4
                    ♡  2
                    ◊  AJ
                    ♣  None
```

If the lead is with South, either the ace of hearts or the ace of diamonds may be played first. If the ace of hearts is first played, East is squeezed and must throw a spade. A spade is led to South's king and the ace of diamonds squeezes West in spades and hearts. If the ace of diamonds is played first, West is squeezed and must throw a spade. North discards the jack of hearts, and at the next trick the ace of hearts squeezes East in spades and diamonds.

In this diagram, if South does not hold a card in the heart suit, the fifth card being in the suit of the double menace, a second situation arises:

(25)

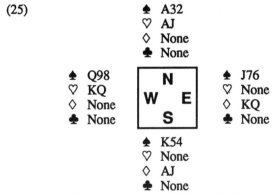

```
                    ♠  A32
                    ♡  AJ
                    ◊  None
                    ♣  None
     ♠  Q98         N          ♠  J76
     ♡  KQ                     ♡  None
     ◊  None     W     E       ◊  KQ
     ♣  None        S          ♣  None
                    ♠  K54
                    ♡  None
                    ◊  AJ
                    ♣  None
```

If South has the lead, the ace of diamonds is played, forcing West to discard a spade. The North hand is entered with the ace of spades, and East

[*] The situations in (24) and (25) were first published in *Bridge Magazine*, January 1953.

is squeezed on the lead of the ace of hearts. Similarly, if North has the lead, the ace of hearts is played, forcing East to discard a spade. The South hand is entered with the king of spades, and West is squeezed on the lead of the ace of diamonds.

The following is a hand which may possibly develop into all three basic positions, (23), (24) and (25), described in this section.

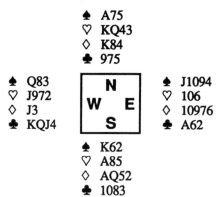

```
                    ♠  A75
                    ♡  KQ43
                    ◇  K84
                    ♣  975
      ♠  Q83        ┌──────────┐        ♠  J1094
      ♡  J972       │    N     │        ♡  106
      ◇  J3         │  W   E   │        ◇  10976
      ♣  KQJ4       │    S     │        ♣  A62
                    └──────────┘
                    ♠  K62
                    ♡  A85
                    ◇  AQ52
                    ♣  1083
```

South is declarer at three no-trumps. The opponents win the first four tricks in clubs, and, at trick five, West leads a heart which is won with dummy's queen. The declarer has eight tricks on top; the ninth trick comes from a squeeze.

On the lead of the fourth club, North - South have three different ways of discarding. Analysis shows that each way of discarding leads to one of the three double-squeeze positions in (23), (24), or (25).

(a) If North discards a spade, and South a heart, the following situation can be arrived at with the lead in the North hand:

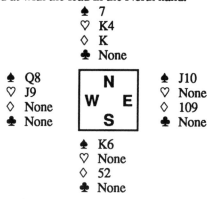

```
                    ♠  7
                    ♡  K4
                    ◇  K
                    ♣  None
      ♠  Q8         ┌──────────┐        ♠  J10
      ♡  J9         │    N     │        ♡  None
      ◇  None       │  W   E   │        ◇  109
      ♣  None       │    S     │        ♣  None
                    └──────────┘
                    ♠  K6
                    ♡  None
                    ◇  52
                    ♣  None
```

56

Here either one of the two red kings may be played first. Each opponent will be squeezed by the lead of the winner of the suit his partner guards. The position is the same as in (23).

The declarer may also play the hand to the following ending with the lead in the North hand:

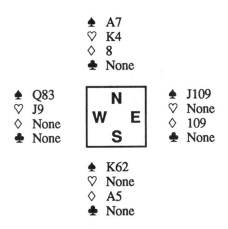

♠ A7
♡ K4
◇ 8
♣ None

♠ Q83   ♠ J109
♡ J9   ♡ None
◇ None   ◇ 109
♣ None   ♣ None

♠ K62
♡ None
◇ A5
♣ None

This is the same situation as in diagram (24).

(b) If North discards a diamond, and South a spade, the following situation can be arrived at with the lead in the South hand:

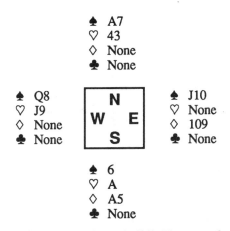

♠ A7
♡ 43
◇ None
♣ None

♠ Q8   ♠ J10
♡ J9   ♡ None
◇ None   ◇ 109
♣ None   ♣ None

♠ 6
♡ A
◇ A5
♣ None

This is again the same situation as in (23). The two red aces play the roles of the squeeze-cards.

The declarer may also play the hand to the following five-card ending, which is of the same type as that in (24).

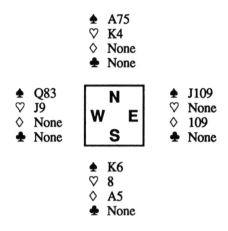

Here the lead will be better in the South hand, so that either the king of hearts or the ace of diamonds may be played first.

(c) If North discards a diamond and South a heart, the following situation can be arrived at:

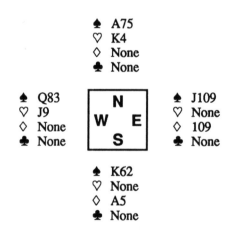

And this is the same situation as in diagram (25).

Note that, if right at the outset West takes only three club tricks instead of four, all the squeezes disappear, and the contract is destined for defeat.

In all the diagrams, (23), (24) and (25), the squeeze is positional—the squeeze fails if the East and West hands are interchanged. Note that in these diagrams each single menace lies in the hand to the left of the opponent who guards the menace suit. The following is an automatic form of the type of squeeze under consideration.

(26)

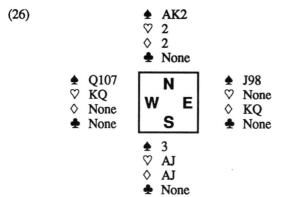

```
              ♠ AK2
              ♡ 2
              ◇ 2
              ♣ None
♠ Q107                        ♠ J98
♡ KQ        N                 ♡ None
◇ None    W     E             ◇ KQ
♣ None        S               ♣ None
              ♠ 3
              ♡ AJ
              ◇ AJ
              ♣ None
```

Suppose the lead is with South. Either opponent may be squeezed first. If the ace of hearts is played first, East is squeezed and has to part with a spade. At the next trick, the lead of the ace of diamonds squeezes West in spades and hearts. Similarly if the ace of diamonds is played first, West is squeezed and has to part with a spade. At the next trick, the lead of the ace of hearts squeezes East in spades and diamonds.

This is illustrated in the following example.

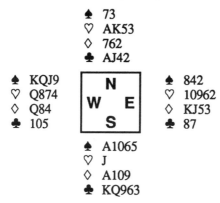

```
              ♠ 73
              ♡ AK53
              ◇ 762
              ♣ AJ42
♠ KQJ9                        ♠ 842
♡ Q874      N                 ♡ 10962
◇ Q84     W     E             ◇ KJ53
♣ 105         S               ♣ 87
              ♠ A1065
              ♡ J
              ◇ A109
              ♣ KQ963
```

The contract is three no-trumps by South. The king and queen of spades are led and allowed to hold. At trick three, West leads a club which is taken by dummy's ace. A small diamond is led, South plays the ten, West's queen winning.

Another club is returned and won by dummy's jack. The declarer takes three more rounds of clubs, leaving this ending:

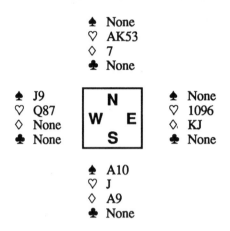

```
              ♠  None
              ♡  AK53
              ◊  7
              ♣  None

♠  J9         ┌───────────┐      ♠  None
♡  Q87        │    N      │      ♡  1096
◊  None       │ W     E   │      ◊  KJ
♣  None       │    S      │      ♣  None
              └───────────┘
              ♠  A10
              ♡  J
              ◊  A9
              ♣  None
```

This is the same situation as in diagram (26).

Observe that if South cashes the ace of spades and ace of diamonds before the last club, the situation becomes:

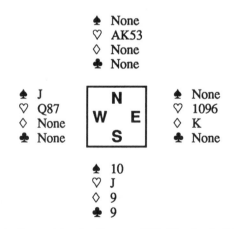

```
              ♠  None
              ♡  AK53
              ◊  None
              ♣  None

♠  J          ┌───────────┐      ♠  None
♡  Q87        │    N      │      ♡  1096
◊  None       │ W     E   │      ◊  K
♣  None       │    S      │      ♣  None
              └───────────┘
              ♠  10
              ♡  J
              ◊  9
              ♣  9
```

And this is the position in diagram (19). The lead of the nine of clubs squeezes West and East simultaneously.

3.6 Double squeezes in two suits

There are several forms of the double squeeze where both opponents are squeezed simultaneously in the same two suits. Such a squeeze requires the presence of an ordinary double menace and a pick-up double menace of the following type:

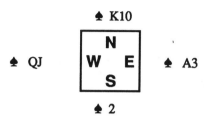

♠ K10

♠ QJ   N
         W   E   ♠ A3
            S

♠ 2

If West discards a spade, the lead of the king of spades forces out East's ace and establishes the ten as a winner. If East discards the three of spades, the ten of spades is led. East has to win and the king is promoted.

Combining such a menace with an ordinary double menace gives two forms of the two-suit double squeeze. This is the first:

(27)

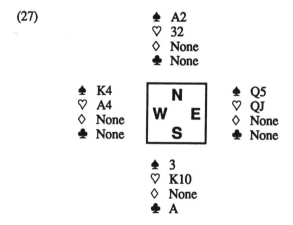

♠ A2
♡ 32
◊ None
♣ None

♠ K4   ♠ Q5
♡ A4   N   ♡ QJ
◊ None W   E   ◊ None
♣ None   S   ♣ None

♠ 3
♡ K10
◊ None
♣ A

South can win two tricks out of four. On the lead of the ace of clubs, the opponents are squeezed simultaneously. If West discards a spade, North throws a heart, and East can do nothing but let go of the jack of hearts. The ace of spades is cashed, and the small heart led from North. South can win one more trick in the heart suit. If West discards the four of hearts, North throws the two of spades. The lead of the ten of hearts forces out West's ace and sets up South's king as a winner.

This end position is demonstrated well by the following hand:

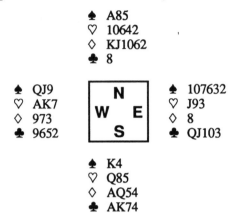

```
              ♠ A85
              ♡ 10642
              ◊ KJ1062
              ♣ 8
  ♠ QJ9         N        ♠ 107632
  ♡ AK7                  ♡ J93
  ◊ 973     W     E      ◊ 8
  ♣ 9652        S        ♣ QJ103
              ♠ K4
              ♡ Q85
              ◊ AQ54
              ♣ AK74
```

The contract is five diamonds by South. West leads the king of hearts and switches to a spade on receiving a discouraging signal from his partner. It seems at first sight as if there are still two losers in hearts and the contract is to go one down. Since the ace of hearts is marked with West, the best hope of making the contract is to find East with the jack and nine of hearts. As the cards lie, by recognizing the position, the following four-card ending can be reached, and the contract fulfilled.

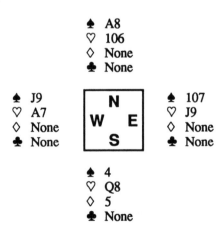

```
              ♠ A8
              ♡ 106
              ◊ None
              ♣ None
  ♠ J9           N        ♠ 107
  ♡ A7                    ♡ J9
  ◊ None     W     E      ◊ None
  ♣ None         S        ♣ None
              ♠ 4
              ♡ Q8
              ◊ 5
              ♣ None
```

The lead of the five of diamonds squeezes both opponents simultaneously.

In the above four-card ending, if the ordinary two-card double menace is in the same hand as the squeeze-card, the special double menace being opposite the squeeze-card, there is no entry to the hand opposite the squeeze-card and the squeeze fails. However, replacing the ordinary two-card double menace with a split three-card double menace, thus providing an entry, enables with situation to exist:

(28)

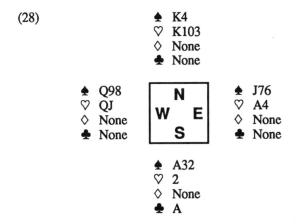

```
                    ♠ K4
                    ♡ K103
                    ◇ None
                    ♣ None
    ♠ Q98                      ♠ J76
    ♡ QJ        N             ♡ A4
    ◇ None   W     E          ◇ None
    ♣ None      S             ♣ None
                    ♠ A32
                    ♡ 2
                    ◇ None
                    ♣ A
```

South can win three tricks out of five. On the lead of the ace of clubs, North discards the three of hearts and the opponents are squeezed simultaneously. If both West and East discard in spades, South can win three tricks in the spade suit; if either opponent discards a heart, a trick will be set up in that suit.

These two-suit double-squeeze situations were first published in my article in the September 1952 edition of *Bridge Magazine*. Later they were included by some bridge writers in their own books and were sometimes called "pinning squeezes".

Diagram (28) is illustrated in the following hand played by South in a contract of three no-trumps.

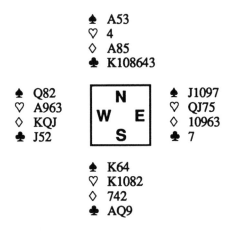

West plays three rounds of diamonds, North's ace winning the third round. The clubs are played out, and, at trick nine, the situation is as follows:

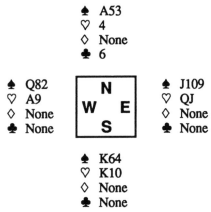

This is the same situation as in diagram (28) with the six of clubs as the squeeze-card in the North hand.

The six of clubs is played, and South discards a spade. If both opponents discard in spades, North-South win three spade tricks. If either opponent discards a heart, the four of hearts is led at the next trick and North-South can set up an extra trick in the heart suit.

Another form of the double squeeze in two suits is obtained by combining a split two-card double menace with a split three-card pick-up double menace:

(29)

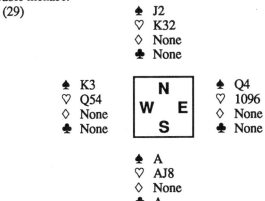

```
              ♠  J2
              ♡  K32
              ◇  None
              ♣  None
  ♠  K3          N          ♠  Q4
  ♡  Q54                     ♡  1096
  ◇  None    W     E         ◇  None
  ♣  None        S           ♣  None
              ♠  A
              ♡  AJ8
              ◇  None
              ♣  A
```

The spade suit in the North-South hands is a split two-card double menace, and the heart suit a split three-card pick-up double menace. On the lead of the ace of clubs, North discards a heart, and both opponents are squeezed simultaneously. If both opponents discard in spades, the jack of spades is established. If West discards a heart, the king, ace and jack of hearts win three tricks in turn. If East discards a heart, the jack of hearts is led. West must cover, the king wins, and all South's cards are winners.

The next hand is an example.

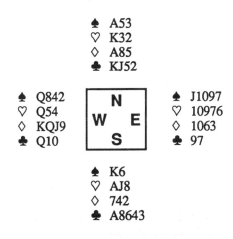

```
              ♠  A53
              ♡  K32
              ◇  A85
              ♣  KJ52
  ♠  Q842         N          ♠  J1097
  ♡  Q54                     ♡  10976
  ◇  KQJ9    W     E         ◇  1063
  ♣  Q10         S           ♣  97
              ♠  K6
              ♡  AJ8
              ◇  742
              ♣  A8643
```

West opens the bidding with one diamond, and the final contract is three no-trumps by South. West leads three rounds of diamonds, North winning the third. It is clear that the three missing queens are all in the West hand. The declarer plays four rounds of clubs to arrive at this position:

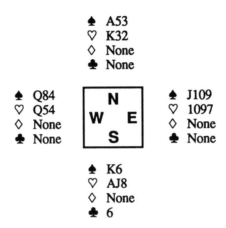

```
                    ♠ A53
                    ♡ K32
                    ◇ None
                    ♣ None
      ♠ Q84         ┌─────────┐      ♠ J109
      ♡ Q54         │    N    │      ♡ 1097
      ◇ None        │  W   E  │      ◇ None
      ♣ None        │    S    │      ♣ None
                    └─────────┘
                    ♠ K6
                    ♡ AJ8
                    ◇ None
                    ♣ 6
```

On the lead of the six of clubs, North lets go of a small heart, and West and East are squeezed simultaneously. The situation would be the same as in diagram (29) if the ace of spades had been played at an earlier stage.

The situation in diagram (29) has an analogue in the simple squeeze:

(30)

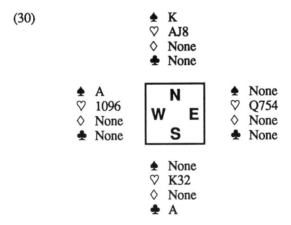

```
                    ♠ K
                    ♡ AJ8
                    ◇ None
                    ♣ None
      ♠ A           ┌─────────┐      ♠ None
      ♡ 1096        │    N    │      ♡ Q754
      ◇ None        │  W   E  │      ◇ None
      ♣ None        │    S    │      ♣ None
                    └─────────┘
                    ♠ None
                    ♡ K32
                    ◇ None
                    ♣ A
```

South leads the ace of clubs, and West is squeezed. If West discards a heart, North throws the king of spades. The ace of hearts is played and the jack of hearts led, forcing East to cover and establishing the eight as an extra winner.

3.7 The nosittej double squeeze

I once watched the following hand played by my dearest friend and favourite partner, the late Mr Tze-kai Kiang, in a rubber game.

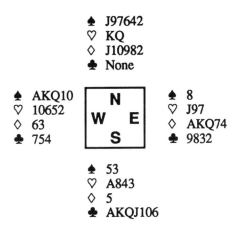

```
                    ♠ J97642
                    ♡ KQ
                    ◊ J10982
                    ♣ None
     ♠ AKQ10                      ♠ 8
     ♡ 10652    ┌─────────┐       ♡ J97
     ◊ 63       │ N       │       ◊ AKQ74
     ♣ 754      │W     E  │       ♣ 9832
                │    S    │
                └─────────┘
                    ♠ 53
                    ♡ A843
                    ◊ 5
                    ♣ AKQJ106
```

At love all, the bidding proceeded:

South	West	North	East
1♣	Pass	1♠	Pass
2♡	Pass	2♠	Pass
3♣	Pass	3◊	Double
3NT	All Pass		

West led the king and queen of spades, while East discarded the seven of diamonds. West then played a diamond to East's queen. East could have taken two more diamond tricks to set the three no-trump contract, but he thought that no harm could be done by returning a heart to dummy's queen.

The declarer, Tze-kai Kiang, instead of immediately cashing the eight obvious tricks, led a diamond from dummy in the hope that something unexpected would happen. East won with the king of diamonds and led a club. Mr Kiang won and led out all his clubs, and, at trick 11, he arrived at this position:[*]

(31)

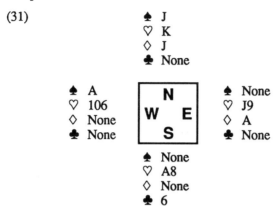

```
                ♠ J
                ♡ K
                ◇ J
                ♣ None

  ♠ A          ┌───────┐      ♠ None
  ♡ 106        │   N   │      ♡ J9
  ◇ None     W │       │ E    ◇ A
  ♣ None       │   S   │      ♣ None
              └───────┘
                ♠ None
                ♡ A8
                ◇ None
                ♣ 6
```

On the lead of the six of clubs, West and East were squeezed simultaneously.

This is really a curiosity in squeeze play. The six of clubs forces West to discard a heart, dummy throws the jack of spades, and East is helpless. If he discards the ace of diamonds, dummy's jack becomes a winner, the king of hearts being the entry to dummy to cash it. If East also discards a heart, South plays the ace and then the eight of hearts to win the last two tricks.

We may call this squeeze a nosittej double squeeze.

This unusual double squeeze very much resembles the ordinary double-squeeze situation in diagram (16) where South has a squeeze-card, North has two one-card menaces, one against each opponent, and the combined hands have a split three-card double menace with the three-card part in the South hand. If we remove a small card from both parts of the split three-card double menace in diagram (16), the result is the same as diagram (31). The blocked heart suit of ace-small opposite king alone in the North-South hands in diagram (31) can be considered as the condensation of a split three-card double menace. The nosittej squeeze works because this condensed menace possesses all the functions of a split three-card menace: the North hand can be entered with the king of hearts, and the South hand has the ace of hearts as an entry, except that the two parts of the menace are both one card shorter than the two parts of a split three-card menace.

[*] *The British Bridge World,* December 1956.

3.8 An example of a double squeeze

The following is a very interesting hand.

North-South game; Dealer North

♠ AKQ2
♡ 42
◇ AK64
♣ KQ7

♠ 943
♡ AK5
◇ Q52
♣ AJ105

The contract is seven no-trumps by South. West leads the jack of diamonds, dummy plays the king, and East discards a heart. South can spread the hand at once (don't do it in a tournament!) and claim thirteen tricks. Why?

South has twelve tricks on top. Just play out the ace, king, queen of spades and the situation will be clear. If the spades break evenly, the two of spades is the thirteenth winner. If West guards the spade suit, a positional simple squeeze in spades and diamonds can be set up against West. The end position would be the same as the one shown in diagram (2). If East has the spade guard, South plays the queen of diamonds, the king of hearts, and four rounds of clubs. On the fourth round of clubs the position would be as follows:

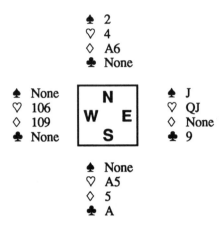

♠ 2
♡ 4
◇ A6
♣ None

♠ None   ♠ J
♡ 106   ♡ QJ
◇ 109   ◇ None
♣ None   ♣ 9

♠ None
♡ A5
◇ 5
♣ A

This is the non-simultaneous positional double-squeeze ending in diagram (17). The lead of the ace of clubs squeezes West in hearts and diamonds. West has to part with a heart, and North lets go of the six of diamonds. At the next trick, the ace of diamonds squeezes East in spades and hearts. It is unnecessary for South to play the hand to the non-simultaneous automatic double-squeeze position in diagram (18) since it is already known that the diamond suit is guarded by West and not East.

Chapter 4

Triple Squeezes

4.1 Basic end positions

When one opponent only is menaced in three suits, a trick or tricks will be set up for the declarer if the entries necessary for the squeeze are available. Among this class of squeeze there are two different types. One is called the triple squeeze in which the declarer can gain only one extra trick if the opponent squeezed discards correctly; the other is the repeated squeeze in which the opponent will be squeezed progressively, and two tricks will be gained by the declarer.

The triple squeeze can be classified as positional or automatic.

The simplest situation of the positional triple-squeeze position consists of two one-card menaces, a two-card menace and a squeeze-card. At the time the squeeze begins, the declarer has just one loser. Such a squeeze is obviously a four-card ending, because the opponent squeezed has four busy cards.

(32)

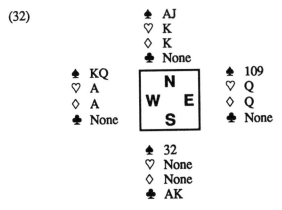

```
              ♠ AJ
              ♡ K
              ◊ K
              ♣ None
   ♠ KQ      ┌─────────┐    ♠ 109
   ♡ A       │    N    │    ♡ Q
   ◊ A       │  W   E  │    ◊ Q
   ♣ None    │    S    │    ♣ None
             └─────────┘
              ♠ 32
              ♡ None
              ◊ None
              ♣ AK
```

South has three winners out of four cards. South leads the ace of clubs and wins an extra trick in the suit in which West discards.

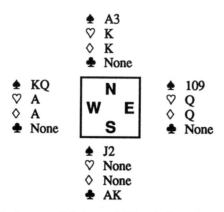

♠ A3
♡ K
◇ K
♣ None

♠ KQ
♡ A
◇ A
♣ None

♠ 109
♡ Q
◇ Q
♣ None

♠ J2
♡ None
◇ None
♣ AK

South leads the ace of clubs, and West is forced to concede a trick to South.

The endings in (32) and (33) are similar to those of the positional simple squeezes in diagrams (2) and (3) in Chapter 2. In both (32) and (33) there is an additional one-card menace as well as an extra club winner. If clubs are trumps, South can ruff North's king of hearts or king of diamonds with a trump at an earlier stage, and the result will be the same as (2) or (3). But in actual play it may be that there is no opportunity to do so. Even if there is the opportunity, it is unnecessary to do it. Playing for a triple squeeze usually offers more chance of success than a simple squeeze.

In diagram (32), if one of the two one-card menaces in the North hand is transferred to the South hand, we obtain the simplest form of the automatic triple squeeze:

(34)

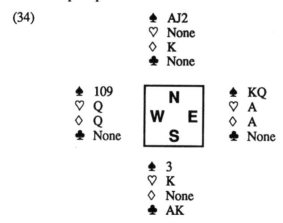

♠ AJ2
♡ None
◇ K
♣ None

♠ 109
♡ Q
◇ Q
♣ None

♠ KQ
♡ A
◇ A
♣ None

♠ 3
♡ K
◇ None
♣ AK

South leads the ace of clubs on which the worthless two of spades is discarded. In whichever suit East may discard, South can always gain an extra trick.

This is the triple squeeze corresponding to the simple squeeze position in diagram (1). Since North has an idle card to discard on the lead of the ace of clubs, the squeeze is automatic.

The following hand is played by South in a contract of five clubs.

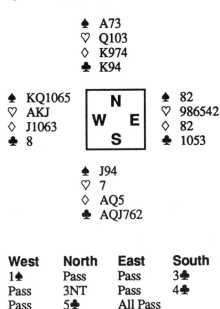

<pre>
              ♠ A73
              ♡ Q103
              ◇ K974
              ♣ K94
  ♠ KQ1065   ♠ 82
  ♡ AKJ   ♡ 986542
  ◇ J1063   ◇ 82
  ♣ 8   ♣ 1053
              ♠ J94
              ♡ 7
              ◇ AQ5
              ♣ AQJ762
</pre>

West	North	East	South
1♠	Pass	Pass	3♣
Pass	3NT	Pass	4♣
Pass	5♣	All Pass	

The opening lead is the king of hearts. At trick two West leads the king of spades, which is allowed to win, and he exits with the eight of clubs. After drawing trumps, the declarer plays three rounds of diamonds, discovering that West has four diamonds to the jack-ten. The declarer then leads the ten of hearts, which South ruffs, leaving this position:

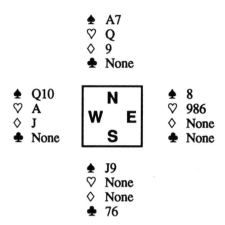

On the lead of the seven of clubs, West is squeezed in three suits. The position is the same as in diagram (33).

In the triple squeezes described above, the squeezing side has only one loser as the squeeze begins. These three situations can be obtained from their simple-squeeze analogues by adding a one-card menace and a fourth-suit winner in each case. Since all three suits are protected by one opponent, the lead of a free-suit winner forces him to make a discard which inevitably concedes a trick to the squeezing side.

In reality, the more useful triple squeezes are those in which the squeezing side has just one winner in the fourth suit.

Corresponding to (32), we have the following situation:

(35)

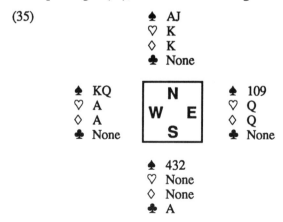

South leads the ace of clubs and gains an extra trick from West's discard.

In this situation, South has two winners and two losers in the four-card ending, and, although the opponents can win a trick after the squeeze is completed, it still gains a trick for the squeezing side.

The situation corresponding to (33) is:

(36)

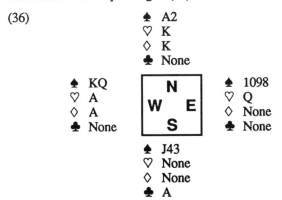

♠ A2
♡ K
◇ K
♣ None

♠ KQ   ♠ 1098
♡ A   ♡ Q
◇ A   ◇ None
♣ None   ♣ None

♠ J43
♡ None
◇ None
♣ A

South leads the ace of clubs, and West is squeezed in three suits. South can win three tricks in this four-card ending.

(35) and (36) are both basic positional triple-squeeze endings. The following is the basic form of the automatic triple squeeze corresponding to (34):

(37)

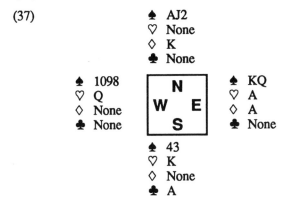

♠ AJ2
♡ None
◇ K
♣ None

♠ 1098   ♠ KQ
♡ Q   ♡ A
◇ None   ◇ A
♣ None   ♣ None

♠ 43
♡ K
◇ None
♣ A

South leads the ace of clubs, and North discards the two of spades. South can always win three tricks in this four-card ending no matter how East chooses to discard.

75

The squeeze is equally effective if the East and West hands are interchanged and is therefore an automatic triple squeeze.

The following hand is played by South in a contract of four hearts.

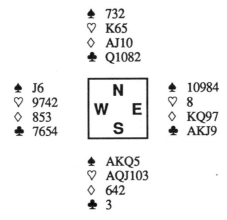

West leads a diamond on which North plays the ten. East wins with the queen and plays the king of clubs. At trick three, East switches to a spade, which South wins. South plays four rounds of hearts and two more rounds of spades to reach the following position:

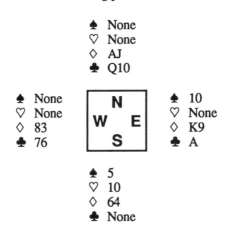

On the lead of the ten of hearts, North discards the ten of clubs, and East is squeezed in three suits. The situation is the same as in diagram (37).

The ending in diagram (32) is a positional triple squeeze against West. If the two-card menace is replaced by a split three-card menace, an automatic triple-squeeze position arises*

(38)

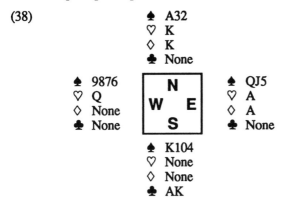

          ♠ A32
          ♡ K
          ◊ K
          ♣ None

♠ 9876   ♠ QJ5
♡ Q   ♡ A
◊ None   ◊ A
♣ None   ♣ None

          ♠ K104
          ♡ None
          ◊ None
          ♣ AK

On the lead of the ace of clubs, North throws the two of spades, and East is squeezed in three suits. There are two winners in the squeeze suit when the squeeze-card is led. The spade suit is a split three-card menace against East.

Note that if either one of the one-card menaces is replaced by a longer menace, the other may be in either hand. If there is only one winner in the squeeze suit, a trick will be lost after the squeeze.

(39)

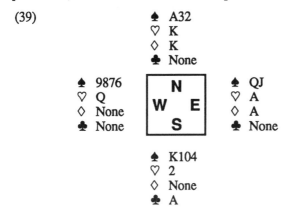

          ♠ A32
          ♡ K
          ◊ K
          ♣ None

♠ 9876   ♠ QJ
♡ Q   ♡ A
◊ None   ◊ A
♣ None   ♣ None

          ♠ K104
          ♡ 2
          ◊ None
          ♣ A

Here either of the one-card menaces may be transferred to the South hand without requiring the other to be increased in length.

* *Bridge Magazine*, September 1952.

The presence of the split three-card menace makes the squeeze positions shown in the last two diagrams automatic, i.e. the squeeze is equally effective if the West and East hands are interchanged.

In the following hand, South is declarer at a contract of six no-trumps.

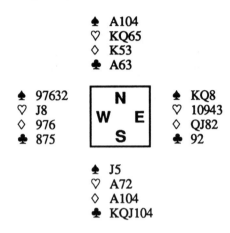

♠ A104
♥ KQ65
◇ K53
♣ A63

♠ 97632   ♠ KQ8
♥ J8   ♥ 10943
◇ 976   ◇ QJ82
♣ 875   ♣ 92

♠ J5
♥ A72
◇ A104
♣ KQJ104

West leads the seven of spades, dummy plays low, East's queen winning. A club is returned.

It seems that the king of spades is in the East hand, but a simple squeeze against East in spades and hearts is not possible, because both menaces lie in front of East. Therefore, the heart winners can be cashed. On the third round of hearts, West discards a spade, showing that the heart guard is in the East hand.

If East has the only stopper in diamonds (queen-jack-small or at least five cards), the diamond suit in the North-South hands can be used as a split three-card menace against East, and a simple squeeze against East in hearts and diamonds, or in spades and diamonds, is effective. In this case a triple squeeze against East (in spades, hearts and diamonds) must also be effective. The end position is as follows:

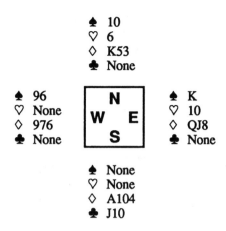

On the lead of the jack of clubs, North discards the three of diamonds, and East is squeezed in three suits. The position is the same as in diagram (38).

Note that if East guards the hearts, but West guards the spades, and the diamonds are guarded by both opponents, a double squeeze works. The end position might be as follows:

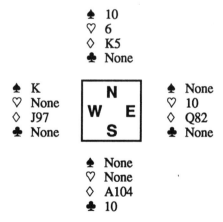

This is the double squeeze position of diagram (16).

Before concluding this section, let us once again consider the situation in diagram (33) although it is a positional triple squeeze against West. But, if clubs are trumps, the South hand is provided with a ruffing entry, and the squeeze becomes automatic:

(40)

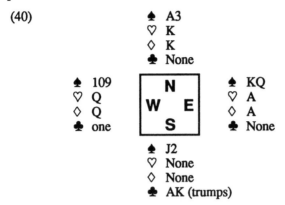

```
            ♠ A3
            ♡ K
            ◇ K
            ♣ None
♠ 109   ┌─────────┐   ♠ KQ
♡ Q     │   N     │   ♡ A
◇ Q     │ W     E │   ◇ A
♣ one   │   S     │   ♣ None
        └─────────┘
            ♠ J2
            ♡ None
            ◇ None
            ♣ AK (trumps)
```

On the lead of the ace of clubs, North lets go of the three of spades. If East discards a spade, the ace of spades is cashed, and a red king is led and ruffed. South makes the last trick with the jack of spades.

4.2 A squeeze that operates at trick one

A squeeze often begins at the eleventh, tenth, or ninth trick of a deal when there are three, four, or five cards remaining. In the extreme case an opponent can be squeezed at the very first trick as the following hand, played by South in a contract of seven no-trumps, demonstrates.

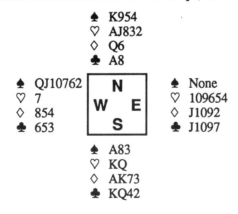

```
                ♠ K954
                ♡ AJ832
                ◇ Q6
                ♣ A8
♠ QJ10762  ┌─────────┐   ♠ None
♡ 7        │   N     │   ♡ 109654
◇ 854      │ W     E │   ◇ J1092
♣ 653      │   S     │   ♣ J1097
           └─────────┘
                ♠ A83
                ♡ KQ
                ◇ AK73
                ♣ KQ42
```

North-South have twelve winners on top. On West lead of the queen of spades, East has to make a discard. In fact, he is squeezed in three suits at trick one. South gains an extra trick in the suit in which East chooses to discard.

If the opening lead is not a spade, the declarer can cash the aces, kings and queens of hearts, diamonds and clubs to arrive at the following ending:[*]

(41)

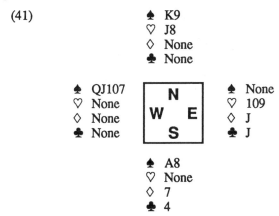

```
                    ♠ K9
                    ♡ J8
                    ◊ None
                    ♣ None

  ♠ QJ107    ┌─────────┐    ♠ None
  ♡ None     │    N    │    ♡ 109
  ◊ None     │ W     E │    ◊ J
  ♣ None     │    S    │    ♣ J
             └─────────┘
                    ♠ A8
                    ♡ None
                    ◊ 7
                    ♣ 4
```

On the lead of the ace of spades, East is squeezed in three suits.

The entry conditions in this triple squeeze are very peculiar. There is no entry in the suit of any of the three single menaces. Either the ace or the king of spades can be used as the squeeze-card. If East discards the jack of diamonds or the jack of clubs, South makes an extra trick with the seven of diamonds or the four of clubs; if East discards a heart, North wins two heart tricks. All the entries in this four-card triple-squeeze position are provided in the free suit.

The squeeze is automatic—West will be squeezed if he holds East's cards.

[*]First published in *Bridge Quarterly* (Chinese), 1991, No.1.

4.3 A squeeze of an opponent in three singletons

Let us study this hand.

Love all; Dealer West

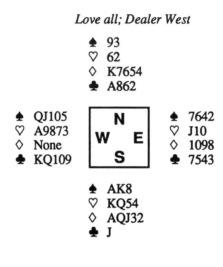

```
            ♠ 93
            ♡ 62
            ◊ K7654
            ♣ A862

  ♠ QJ105     ┌───────┐     ♠ 7642
  ♡ A9873     │   N   │     ♡ J10
  ◊ None      │ W   E │     ◊ 1098
  ♣ KQ109     │   S   │     ♣ 7543
              └───────┘
            ♠ AK8
            ♡ KQ54
            ◊ AQJ32
            ♣ J
```

West	North	East	South
1♣	Pass	Pass	Double
1♡	Pass	Pass	3◊
Pass	4◊	Pass	5◊
Pass	6◊	All Pass	

West leads the king of clubs, dummy's ace winning. Dummy leads a club, which South ruffs. South plays the ace and queen of diamonds, West discarding a heart and a spade. At trick five, South leads the king of hearts, which is allowed to hold. South continues with the queen of hearts, West's ace winning. At trick seven, West leads the nine of hearts, dummy ruffs with the king of diamonds, and East discards a club. A club is led from dummy, South ruffing with the three of diamonds. South then wins the ninth and tenth tricks with the ace and king of spades.

The situation at trick 11 is very interesting:

(42)

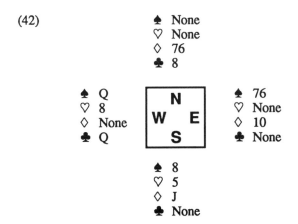

```
            ♠ None
            ♡ None
            ◇ 76
            ♣ 8

  ♠ Q      ┌─────────┐    ♠ 76
  ♡ 8      │    N    │    ♡ None
  ◇ None   │ W     E │    ◇ 10
  ♣ Q      │    S    │    ♣ None
           └─────────┘
            ♠ 8
            ♡ 5
            ◇ J
            ♣ None
```

West has three singletons and all are master cards. South's eight of spades threatens West's queen of spades, the five of hearts threatens West's eight of hearts, and North's eight of clubs threatens West's queen of clubs. Now the jack of diamonds is led, drawing East's ten of trumps and squeezing West in three suits. If West discards the spade or the heart, South's eight of spades or five of hearts becomes a winner. If West discards the club, the North hand is entered with the last trump and the eight of clubs is made.

This triple squeeze of West in three singletons is one of the rare situations in squeeze endings.

The squeeze is automatic—if the West and East hands are interchanged, East will be squeezed in three singletons.

4.4 Double triple squeezes

Occasionally, at the time the squeeze-card is led, both opponents are simultaneously squeezed in all three suits.

When this is the case the squeeze is called a "double triple squeeze". This kind of squeeze depends on the existence of an ordinary double menace and two pick-up double menaces as described in Section 1.2.

The following are four different double-triple-squeeze end positions.[*]

(43)

	North	
♠	None	
♡	A2	
◊	K102	
♣	None	

West		East
♠ A	**N**	♠ K
♡ K3	**W E**	♡ J4
◊ QJ	**S**	◊ A4
♣ None		♣ None

	South
♠	Q
♡	Q10
◊	3
♣	A

(44)

	North
♠	J2
♡	A2
◊	32
♣	None

West		East
♠ K3	**N**	♠ Q4
♡ K3	**W E**	♡ J4
◊ A4	**S**	◊ QJ
♣ None		♣ None

	South
♠	A
♡	Q10
◊	K10
♣	A

(45)

	North
♠	A2
♡	Q10
◊	32
♣	None

West		East
♠ Q5	**N**	♠ K4
♡ J4	**W E**	♡ K3
◊ A4	**S**	◊ QJ
♣ None		♣ None

	South
♠	3
♡	A2
◊	K10
♣	A

[*] *Bridge Magazine,* September 1952.

(46)

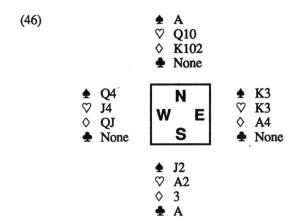

```
              ♠  A
              ♡  Q10
              ◇  K102
              ♣  None

  ♠  Q4              ┌─────────┐         ♠  K3
  ♡  J4              │    N    │         ♡  K3
  ◇  QJ              │  W   E  │         ◇  A4
  ♣  None            │    S    │         ♣  None
                     └─────────┘

              ♠  J2
              ♡  A2
              ◇  3
              ♣  A
```

In each of these situations the ace of clubs is the squeeze-card and tricks will be lost after the squeeze. When the ace of clubs is led, North discards the two of diamonds in each case, and the opponents are squeezed simultaneously.

In diagram (43), for example, South can win two tricks out of five cards. If West throws the three of hearts on the lead of the ace of clubs, North's ace of hearts drops the king, and South's queen becomes a winner. If West throws the jack of diamonds, the three of diamonds is led. North's king loses to East's ace and the ten is established. If West discards the ace of spades, East is squeezed. He cannot discard the king of spades. If he throws the four of hearts, the queen of hearts is led. West must cover, the ace wins and South's ten becomes top in the suit. If he throws the four of diamonds, the three of diamonds is led, North plays the ten, and East has to win with the ace. North's king is now established.

Hence, whatever the opponents might discard, an additional trick can always be set up for North-South.

Similarly, in diagrams (44), (45) and (46), the opponents cannot both discard in spades on the lead of the ace of clubs, yet if either opponent discards in hearts or diamonds a trick will be set up for North-South in the suit in which the discard is made.

A further double-triple-squeeze ending can be set up by introducing a split three-card pick-up double menace. In this case the two-card double menace can be replaced by a one-card double menace.

(47)

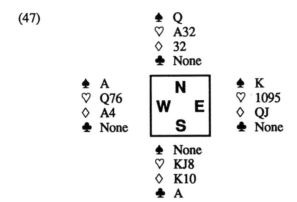

```
                    ♠ Q
                    ♡ A32
                    ◊ 32
                    ♣ None
    ♠ A            N            ♠ K
    ♡ Q76                       ♡ 1095
    ◊ A4      W        E        ◊ QJ
    ♣ None         S            ♣ None
                    ♠ None
                    ♡ KJ8
                    ◊ K10
                    ♣ A
```

The ace of clubs is the squeeze-card. The queen of spades in the opposite hand is a one-card double menace against both opponents. The heart and diamond suits in the North-South hands are pick-up double menaces.

On the lead of the ace of clubs, North discards a diamond. If West throws a heart, North and South win three tricks in hearts with the ace, king and jack of hearts. If West throws the four of diamonds, South leads the ten of diamonds, and West can win his two aces and no more. If West throws the ace of spades on the ace of clubs, East is squeezed. He cannot discard the king of spades. A heart discard permits South to play the jack of hearts, forcing West to cover and setting up South's eight as a new winner. A diamond discard enables South to lead the king of diamonds and establishes a winner in the diamond suit.

In the following hand, South is declarer at a contract of three no-trumps.

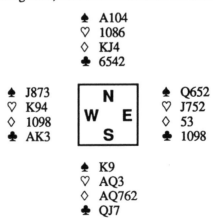

```
                    ♠ A104
                    ♡ 1086
                    ◊ KJ4
                    ♣ 6542
    ♠ J873           N           ♠ Q652
    ♡ K94                        ♡ J752
    ◊ 1098     W        E        ◊ 53
    ♣ AK3            S           ♣ 1098
                    ♠ K9
                    ♡ AQ3
                    ◊ AQ762
                    ♣ QJ7
```

West leads the ten of diamonds, dummy's king winning. South tries the finesse of the queen of hearts, but West wins with the king and leads the nine of diamonds, won by dummy's jack. Dummy leads a club to the eight, jack and king. At trick five, West leads the eight of diamonds to South's queen. South plays the king of spades and another diamond, leaving this ending:

```
              ♠ A10
              ♡ 108
              ◇ None
              ♣ 65
  ♠ J8                        ♠ Q6
  ♡ 94       ┌─────────┐      ♡ J7
  ◇ None     │    N    │      ◇ None
  ♣ A3       │  W   E  │      ♣ 109
             │    S    │
             └─────────┘
              ♠ 9
              ♡ A3
              ◇ 7
              ♣ Q7
```

On the lead of the seven of diamonds, North discards a club and both opponents are simultaneously squeezed in three suits. The situation is the same as in diagram (45). The spade suit in the North-South hands is an ordinary two-card double menace, and the heart and club suits are two pick-up double menaces.

Chapter 5

Repeated Squeezes

Up to now, all the squeezes discussed can gain one extra trick for the squeezing side. However, if the only stoppers of three suits are concentrated in one opponent's hand, and if the declarer's three menaces are appropriately situated then that two extra tricks can be set up for the declarer irrespective of the opponent's defence. This squeeze is called a "repeated squeeze".

The principle of a repeated squeeze can be stated as follows. When a squeeze-card is played, the opponent is forced to abandon a stopper in one of the three suits which he alone can guard. This gives the declarer a new winner.

This newly established winner is used as a squeeze-card to execute a second squeeze against the same opponent in the remaining two suits. The declarer thus gains a second additional trick from the squeeze.

5.1 Positional repeated squeezes

First let us study the following hand.

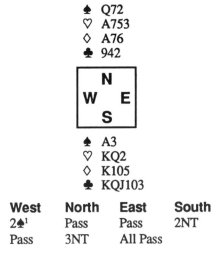

	♠ Q72
	♡ A753
	◊ A76
	♣ 942

	♠ A3
	♡ KQ2
	◊ K105
	♣ KQJ103

West	North	East	South
2♠[1]	Pass	Pass	2NT
Pass	3NT	All Pass	

[1]Weak two

West leads the jack of hearts, which is taken by South's queen. South leads the jack of clubs, West discarding the eight of spades. After taking the ace of clubs, East leads the four of spades.

South has ten winners and three losers. Since West has made a weak-two-spade opening bid, and East has shown up with the ace of clubs, the unseen seven high card points are likely to be all in the West hand. North's queen of spades and seven of hearts and South's ten of diamonds are probably all single menaces against West. Now, both North and South have sufficient entries, so it is possible that a repeated squeeze will work, and the declarer can gain two extra tricks. Of course, if the hearts break evenly, a simple squeeze will be enough.

Thus the declarer plays the ace when East leads the four of spades.

Suppose the spade, heart and diamond suits are all stopped by West, and East cannot guard any one of these suits. In order to see the situation more clearly, we can cash the ace of diamonds and the king of hearts before running the clubs. On the last round of clubs this is the five-card ending:

(48)

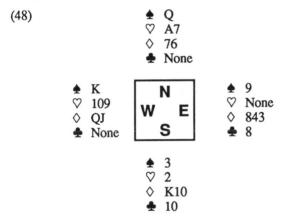

```
                    ♠ Q
                    ♡ A7
                    ◇ 76
                    ♣ None

   ♠ K                            ♠ 9
   ♡ 109          N               ♡ None
   ◇ QJ        W     E            ◇ 843
   ♣ None         S               ♣ 8

                    ♠ 3
                    ♡ 2
                    ◇ K10
                    ♣ 10
```

South leads the ten of clubs and West is squeezed in three suits. North has an idle card to discard—the six of diamonds.

If West discards the king of spades, South leads the two of hearts to the ace and then plays the queen of spades. This card is a new squeeze-card which squeezes West in hearts and diamonds and gains a second additional trick for South.

If West discards a heart, North's ace and seven of hearts take two tricks. On the lead of the seven of hearts, South throws the three of spades, and West is simple-squeezed in spades and diamonds.

If West discards the jack of diamonds, South plays the king of diamonds, dropping West's lone queen. South then leads the ten of diamonds, and West is again squeezed in spades and hearts.

We see that in each case there are two successive squeezes against West, and South can always make two additional tricks.

The position in (48) is a basic form of the positional repeated squeeze. It works only against West. The requirements are very easy to remember: South has the squeeze-card; there are two two-card menaces against West, one in the South hand and one in the North hand; a one-card menace against West lies over West.

If the East and West hands are interchanged, the squeeze will give South one extra winner. He cannot gain two extra tricks provided that East discards correctly. On the lead of the ten of clubs, East simply lets go of a diamond and preserves the stoppers in the suits of the two menaces which lie in front of him, then the second squeeze does not exist.

Here is another hand.

North-South game; Dealer South

```
        ♠ 92
        ♡ 8652
        ◇ AK53
        ♣ KQ2
      ┌─────────┐
      │    N    │
      │  W   E  │
      │    S    │
      └─────────┘
        ♠ AQ8
        ♡ AJ
        ◇ Q72
        ♣ J10943
```

South	West	North	East
1NT	Pass	2◇ [1]	2♠
3NT	All Pass		

[1] Forcing Stayman

West leads the six of spades to the two, king and ace. A club is lost to East's ace and East returns the jack of spades, which is taken by South's queen.

South has ten top winners. If East has the only stoppers in all three suits, a repeated squeeze against East is possible. South can cash the king and queen of diamonds and then play the club winners. On the last round of clubs the situation is:

(49)

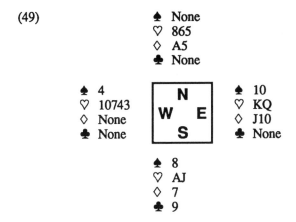

               ♠ None
               ♡ 865
               ◊ A5
               ♣ None

♠ 4   ♠ 10
♡ 10743   ♡ KQ
◊ None   ◊ J10
♣ None   ♣ None

               ♠ 8
               ♡ AJ
               ◊ 7
               ♣ 9

South leads the nine of clubs, North discards a heart, and East is squeezed in three suits.

If East discards the ten of spades, South leads the eight of spades on which North throws another heart, and East is again squeezed in hearts and diamonds.

If East discards the queen of hearts, South plays the ace and jack of hearts. On the lead of the jack of hearts, East is again squeezed in spades and diamonds.

If East discards the ten of diamonds, South plays the ace and five of diamonds. On the lead of the five of diamonds, East is again squeezed in spades and hearts.

Like (48), the position in (49) is also a basic form of the positional repeated squeeze. This squeeze is effective against East. In a sense, the two diagrams, (48) and (49), are symmetrical. The requirements of (49) are also similar to those of (48): South has the squeeze-card; the North and South hands each contain a two-card menace against East; a one-card menace against East lies over East.

If the West and East hands are interchanged, and if West discards correctly, South can win one extra trick but not two. (Why?)

Another basic positional-repeated-squeeze ending occurs when there are two split three-card menaces with both three-card parts in the same hand as the squeeze-card and a one-card menace situated opposite the squeeze-card:

(50)

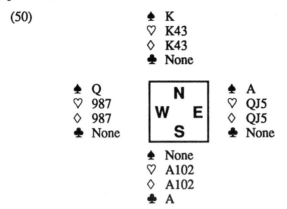

        ♠ K
        ♡ K43
        ◇ K43
        ♣ None

♠ Q   ♠ A
♡ 987   ♡ QJ5
◇ 987   ◇ QJ5
♣ None   ♣ None

        ♠ None
        ♡ A102
        ◇ A102
        ♣ A

On the lead of the ace of clubs, North throws a heart or a diamond and East is squeezed in three suits. If East discards the ace of spades, the North hand is entered with a red king and the king of spades led, squeezing East in hearts and diamonds. If East discards a heart or a diamond, South wins three tricks in the discarded suit. On the third round, East is again squeezed in the remaining two suits.

This situation is therefore a positional repeated squeeze against the opponent to the right of the squeeze-card.

The following hand is an example.

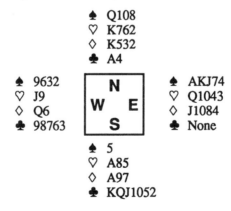

        ♠ Q108
        ♡ K762
        ◇ K532
        ♣ A4

♠ 9632   ♠ AKJ74
♡ J9   ♡ Q1043
◇ Q6   ◇ J1084
♣ 98763   ♣ None

        ♠ 5
        ♡ A85
        ◇ A97
        ♣ KQJ1052

The contract is six clubs by South, East having made an opening bid of one spade. West leads a spade, dummy plays the eight, and East's jack wins. East continues with the king of spades, which South ruffs. South plays off five rounds of clubs, and, on the fifth round, the position is the same as in diagram (50). Twelve tricks are made through a repeated squeeze against East.

Now consider diagram (50). If the positions of the menaces in the North and South hands are reversed, a new ending is obtained:

(51)

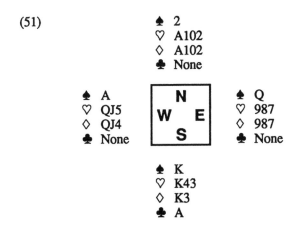

```
              ♠ 2
              ♡ A102
              ◊ A102
              ♣ None
♠ A                        ♠ Q
♡ QJ5       ┌─────┐        ♡ 987
◊ QJ4       │  N  │        ◊ 987
♣ None      │W   E│        ♣ None
            │  S  │
            └─────┘
              ♠ K
              ♡ K43
              ◊ K3
              ♣ A
```

On the lead of the ace of clubs, West is squeezed in three suits. If West discards the ace of spades, he will be subjected to a simple positional squeeze on the lead of the king of spades. If West discards a heart or a diamond, South wins three tricks in that suit, and, on the third round, West is again squeezed—the position reducing to a simple automaic squeeze.

The ending in (51) is a positional repeated squeeze against West. If East holds West's cards, he can discard the ace of spades on the ace of clubs and the squeeze cannot be repeated.

5.2 Automatic repeated squeezes

Consider the following hand.

Game all; Dealer North

    ♠ A963
    ♡ A108
    ◊ A103
    ♣ AQ9

    ♠ K5
    ♡ J54
    ◊ J72
    ♣ KJ1083

North	South
1♣[1]	1NT
2♣[2]	2NT
3NT	Pass

[1] Precision, 16+
[2] Stayman

West leads the queen of spades to the three, four and king. South leads the four of hearts to the three, ten and king. East returns the two of clubs, South's ten wins, and West follows with the seven. South then leads the two of diamonds to the eight, ten and king. At trick five, East returns another club, West discards the two of spades, and North wins with the ace of clubs.

South has nine top winners and has lost two tricks. If West holds the queen of hearts and the queen of diamonds in addition to five or six spades, South can cash the two red aces in dummy, return to the South hand with the king of clubs and play another club winner to arrive at this position:

(52)

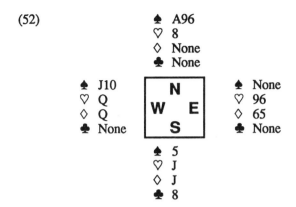

South leads the eight of clubs, North discards the eight of hearts, and West is squeezed in three suits. If West discards a spade, North wins three spade tricks, and if West discards the queen of hearts or the queen of diamonds, South plays the jack of hearts or the jack of diamonds, and West is again squeezed in the remaining two suits.

This is another basic form of the automatic repeated squeeze. East will be squeezed if the West and East hands are interchanged.

The ace-nine-six of spades in the North hand is an extended two-card menace against West. If the opponent squeezed discards a spade, two extra tricks are at once set up for South in the suit. The automatic-repeated-squeeze position in (52) is formed by combining an extended two-card menace with two one-card menaces.

This is the complete deal:

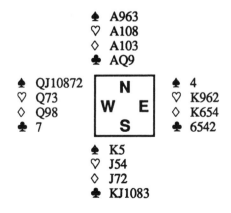

The following is another automatic-repeated-squeeze position:

(53)

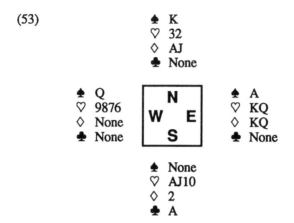

```
              ♠ K
              ♡ 32
              ◊ AJ
              ♣ None

♠ Q        ┌─────────┐    ♠ A
♡ 9876     │    N    │    ♡ KQ
◊ None     │  W   E  │    ◊ KQ
♣ None     │    S    │    ♣ None
           └─────────┘
              ♠ None
              ♡ AJ10
              ◊ 2
              ♣ A
```

North's king of spades is a one-card menace against the ace of spades. If West holds the only stoppers in spades, hearts and diamonds, then the North-South cards form an ideal combination for a repeated squeeze against West. All the requirements are satisfied for the squeeze in diagram (48). But now it is East, and not West, who has the only stoppers in the three suits. In addition, the position in (53) differs from that of (48) in that the heart suit is an extended two-card menace instead of being an ordinary two-card menace. Since this is a five-card ending, the opponent who alone guards the three suits can only retain two cards in the heart suit (the king and queen). If he discards a heart, South gains two additional tricks at once with the jack-ten of hearts. Like the situation in (52), the presence of the extended menace makes the above situation an automatic repeated squeeze.

On the lead of the ace of clubs, North discards the worthless two of hearts. If East discards a heart, both the jack and ten of hearts become winners. If East discards the ace of spades, South leads the two of diamonds to the ace and plays North's king of spades. East is again squeezed in hearts and diamonds. If East discards a diamond, South plays the ace and then the jack of diamonds, and East is again squeezed in spades and hearts.

If the East and West hands are interchanged, the result is the same. The repeated squeeze is equally effective against West.

The following hand is played by South in a contract of three no-trumps after East's opening bid of one spade.

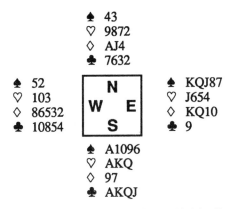

```
              ♠  43
              ♡  9872
              ◊  AJ4
              ♣  7632
  ♠  52                        ♠  KQJ87
  ♡  103         N             ♡  J654
  ◊  86532    W     E          ◊  KQ10
  ♣  10854       S             ♣  9
              ♠  A1096
              ♡  AKQ
              ◊  97
              ♣  AKQJ
```

West leads the five of spades to East's jack which is allowed to win. East leads the king of diamonds, declarer ducking. At trick three, East switches to the nine of clubs. South plays three rounds of clubs followed by three rounds of hearts to arrive at this position:

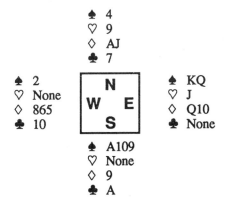

```
              ♠  4
              ♡  9
              ◊  AJ
              ♣  7
  ♠  2                         ♠  KQ
  ♡  None         N            ♡  J
  ◊  865       W     E         ◊  Q10
  ♣  10           S            ♣  None
              ♠  A109
              ♡  None
              ◊  9
              ♣  A
```

South has three winners out of five cards. The ace of clubs is led and East is subjected to an automatic repeated squeeze. North-South's spade suit is an extended two-card menace against East's king-queen of spades. The position is the same as in diagram (53). South eventually makes eleven tricks.

A further automatic-repeated-squeeze ending can be obtained by introducing an extended split three-card menace.

(54)

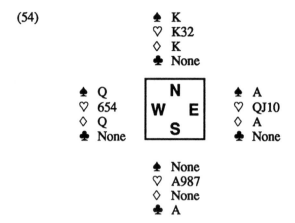

```
                    ♠ K
                    ♡ K32
                    ◊ K
                    ♣ None
    ♠ Q          ┌─────────┐      ♠ A
    ♡ 654        │    N    │      ♡ QJ10
    ◊ Q          │ W     E │      ◊ A
    ♣ None       │    S    │      ♣ None
                 └─────────┘
                    ♠ None
                    ♡ A987
                    ◊ None
                    ♣ A
```

North-South's heart suit is an extended split three-card menace against East's queen-jack-ten of hearts. In addition, North has two one-card menaces against East.

On the lead of the ace of clubs, North throws a heart and East is squeezed. If he discards a heart, North-South win four tricks in hearts. If he discards an ace, the North hand is entered with the king of hearts, and the newly established king of spades or king of diamonds is led and East is again squeezed.

Since the second squeeze is always automatic, the situation in diagram (54) is an automatic repeated squeeze.

The next hand is an example.

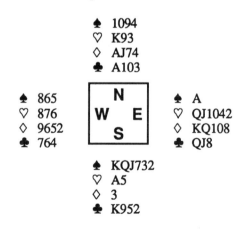

```
                    ♠ 1094
                    ♡ K93
                    ◊ AJ74
                    ♣ A103
    ♠ 865        ┌─────────┐      ♠ A
    ♡ 876        │    N    │      ♡ QJ1042
    ◊ 9652       │ W     E │      ◊ KQ108
    ♣ 764        │    S    │      ♣ QJ8
                 └─────────┘
                    ♠ KQJ732
                    ♡ A5
                    ◊ 3
                    ♣ K952
```

East opens one heart and South becomes declarer at a contract of six spades. West leads the eight of hearts which South's ace wins. The king of spades is led, taken by East's ace. East returns the king of diamonds which is won with dummy's ace. After drawing trumps, a diamond is led from dummy and ruffed by South. The king of hearts is played and another diamond led and ruffed. This is the position at trick nine:

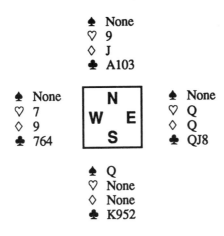

```
                 ♠ None
                 ♡ 9
                 ◊ J
                 ♣ A103
    ♠ None      ┌─────────┐   ♠ None
    ♡ 7         │    N    │   ♡ Q
    ◊ 9         │  W   E  │   ◊ Q
    ♣ 764       │    S    │   ♣ QJ8
                └─────────┘
                 ♠ Q
                 ♡ None
                 ◊ None
                 ♣ K952
```

On the lead of the queen of spades, North discards a club and East is squeezed. The discard of a red queen permits the declarer to enter dummy with the ace of clubs and lead the new winner in hearts or diamonds, squeezing East again in the remaining two suits. The discard of a club concedes two extra club tricks to South. The situation is the same as in diagram (54).

To unearth a new repeated-squeeze end position had been a dream of mine for many years. It was accomplished in a hand similar to the following one, and I was very proud of my work.

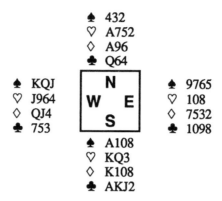

The contract is six no-trumps by South. West leads the king of spades, South ducks and wins the spade continuation with the ace.

The declarer has only ten tricks on top. In order to make the contract, if the hearts fail to break evenly, a repeated squeeze is the only hope. The spade suit is stopped by West. If a repeated squeeze is to be successful, it must be against West.

We know that in an ordinary positional repeated squeeze there must be two two-card menaces and one one-card menace, the latter being situated on the left of the opponent squeezed; while in an automatic repeated squeeze one of the menaces must be extended so that two extra tricks are immediately set up in that suit if the opponent squeezed unguards it. But in the above hand the situation is not so.

South's ten of spades is a one-card menace against West. Unfortunately it is wrongly placed: it lies in front of West. Nevertheless, South cashes the king and queen of hearts and plays three rounds of clubs. The situation at trick eight is:

(55)

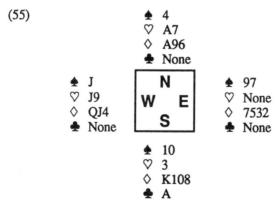

The ace of clubs is now led, North throwing the worthless four of spades. If West discards his jack of spades, South's ten of spades squeezes him again in hearts and diamonds. If West discards a heart, the ace and seven of hearts are played, South lets go of a diamond and West is again squeezed in spades and diamonds. And if West diacards a diamond, South wins the ace, king and ten of diamonds in turn, squeezing West again in spades and hearts.

Since the second squeeze is always automatic regardless of which suit West unguards at the first squeeze, the situation is an automatic repeated squeeze, and East will be squeezed if he holds West's cards.

This diagram is a brand new repeated-squeeze position.[*] The special feature of the diamond suit, which is a split three-card menace with three cards in both hands, compensates for the misplacing of the one-card spade menace and hence makes the repeated squeeze automatic.

Note that a premature discard of a diamond in either the North or South hand may destroy the second squeeze.

It was more than thirty years after the discovery of the squeeze position in diagram (55) that I found it had a parallel.

(56)
```
              ♠ 104
              ♡ 3
              ◇ A96
              ♣ None
♠ 97                        ♠ J
♡ None    ┌─────────┐       ♡ J9
◇ 7532    │    N    │       ◇ QJ4
♣ None    │ W     E │       ♣ None
          │    S    │
          └─────────┘
              ♠ None
              ♡ A7
              ◇ K108
              ♣ A
```

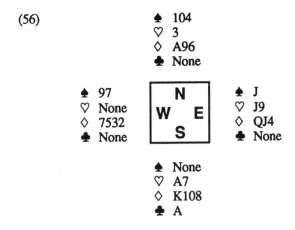

---

[*]This squeeze position was first published in *Bridge Magazine*, February 1957. See also *The Official Encyclopedia of Bridge*, 4th ed., 1984, p.346, shown in diagram (56).

On the lead of the ace of clubs, North discards the four of spades. If East discards the jack of spades, South cashes the king and ace of diamonds, and leads the jack of spades, squeezing East again in simple-automatic fashion in diamonds and hearts. If East discards a heart, the ace and seven of hearts are played, North throwing a diamond, and East is again squeezed automatically in spades and diamonds. If East discards a diamond, South plays three rounds of diamonds, ending in the North hand. On the third round of diamonds, East is again squeezed in spades and hearts.

In this situation, as in the preceding one, the one-card menace (the ten of spades) lies in front of the opponent squeezed. Yet it is a perfect repeated-squeeze situation. It is an automatic repeated squeeze since the second squeeze is always automatic. Once again the presence of the special split three-card menace turns a positional repeated squeeze into an automatic one.

The situations in diagrams (48) to (54) are the seven basic forms of the repeated squeeze. The positions in diagrams (55) and (56) are two basic situations which the author contributed to the repeated squeeze. If we examine these nine end positions carefully, we would always find in each one an artistic beauty.

5.3 Double repeated squeezes

The following situation is known as "Bonney's squeeze":

(57)

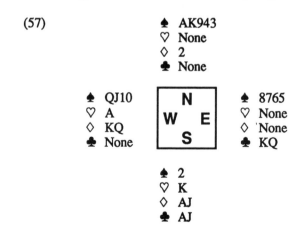

```
                    ♠ AK943
                    ♡ None
                    ◊ 2
                    ♣ None

   ♠ QJ10       ┌─────────┐      ♠ 8765
   ♡ A          │    N    │      ♡ None
   ◊ KQ         │ W     E │      ◊ None
   ♣ None       │    S    │      ♣ KQ
                └─────────┘
                    ♠ 2
                    ♡ K
                    ◊ AJ
                    ♣ AJ
```

This situation is a combination of a simple squeeze against East and a triple squeeze against West.

If the ace of diamonds is first played, East is simple-squeezed and must discard a spade. This play of the ace of diamonds does not produce an immediate winner for South, but East can no longer guard the spades and, at the next trick, the lead of the ace of clubs begins a repeated squeeze against West. The situation is similar to that of diagram (52), except that the spade suit here is an extended three-card menace against West after a spade is discarded by East.

If the ace of clubs is played first, West is triple-squeezed. His best discard is a spade, which, for the time being, does not give South the chance of a second squeeze since the fourth spade trick is protected by East. However, at the next trick, South plays the ace of diamonds, and East is simple-squeezed in spades and clubs.

The following hand is an example.

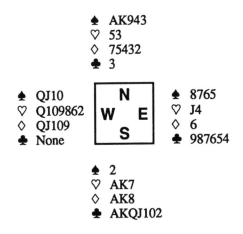

♠ AK943
♡ 53
◇ 75432
♣ 3

♠ QJ10   ♠ 8765
♡ Q109862   ♡ J4
◇ QJ109   ◇ 6
♣ None   ♣ 987654

♠ 2
♡ AK7
◇ AK8
♣ AKQJ102

The contract is six no-trumps by South. West leads the queen of diamonds, declarer's king winning. Four rounds of clubs and the ace and king of hearts are played to arrive at the following position:

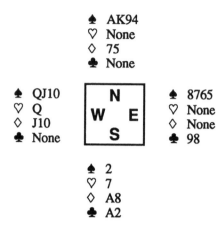

This is the same double-repeated-squeeze position as shown in diagram (57). The declarer eventually wins all thirteen tricks.

The following hand is another example of a double repeated squeeze.[*]

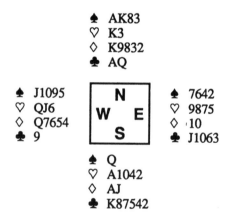

The contract is seven no-trumps by South. West leads the jack of spades. The first seven tricks are won with the queen of spades, the ace and queen of clubs, the ace and king of spades (South discards two clubs), and the ace and jack of diamonds. The six-card end position is:

[*] *Bridge Quarterly* (Chinese), 1987, No. 2.

(58)

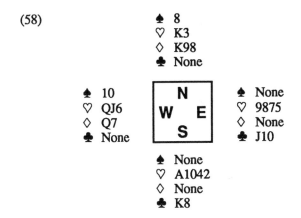

```
              ♠ 8
              ♡ K3
              ◊ K98
              ♣ None
♠ 10          ┌─────────┐      ♠ None
♡ QJ6         │   N     │      ♡ 9875
◊ Q7          │ W     E │      ◊ None
♣ None        │   S     │      ♣ J10
              └─────────┘
              ♠ None
              ♡ A1042
              ◊ None
              ♣ K8
```

The heart suit in the North-South hands is a split three-card menace against West. If East can be forced to discard a heart, it becomes an extended split three-card menace against West. If West can be forced to discard a heart, it becomes a split four-card menace against East.

The king of clubs is led. If West discards a spade or a diamond, a second squeeze will operate against him at a later trick. West therefore discards a heart on the lead of the king of clubs; North lets go of a diamond. The North hand is entered with the king of hearts, and the king of diamonds is led. At this trick, East is squeezed in hearts and clubs.

This is a variation of (57). West is subjected to a triple squeeze and East to a simple squeeze.

Chapter 6

Ruffing Squeezes

In the squeeze situations described in the preceding chapters, the ruffing power of a trump suit has not come into use. The only exceptions are the positions in diagrams (40) and (42), where an opponent is squeezed in three suits and the trump card is used mainly as a ruffing entry to the hand which contains a winner set up by an opponent's forced discard. However, the capacity to ruff can cause new trouble to the opponents. For example, assume that South is in a contract where clubs are trumps. Suppose North has the queen-two of hearts, East has ace-king doubleton, and South is now void in hearts. If East is forced to discard the king of hearts, the two of hearts can be led from North for South to ruff. This play will kill East's ace and establish North's queen as a winner. North's queen-two of hearts is called a "ruffing menace" against East's ace-king of hearts.

This ruffing menace forces the opponent to preserve two cards in the heart suit, otherwise a ruff clears his remaining master card.

Combining a ruffing menace with a menace of another type produces a ruffing squeeze under certain conditions.

6.1 Single ruffing squeezes

Let us study this hand.

North-South game; Dealer North

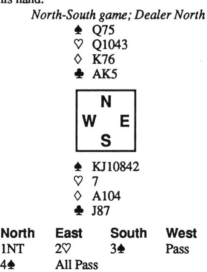

```
          ♠  Q75
          ♡  Q1043
          ◇  K76
          ♣  AK5

               N
            W     E
               S

          ♠  KJ10842
          ♡  7
          ◇  A104
          ♣  J87
```

North	East	South	West
1NT	2♡	3♠	Pass
4♠	All Pass		

West leads the jack of hearts, dummy covers with the queen, and East's king wins. East returns the nine of spades to West's ace. West leads the queen of diamonds, which is allowed to hold. At trick four, West leads the three of clubs, dummy's king taking the trick. Dummy leads a small heart, South ruffs high, and West follows with the nine of hearts. After drawing trumps, South cashes the ace of diamonds and plays on spades.

East has overcalled two hearts. West has shown seven high card points: the ace of spades, the queen of diamonds, and the jack of hearts. He probably has the jack-nine of diamonds as well. Therefore, the queen of clubs is likely to be with East. Besides, it is quite obvious that East has the ace of hearts.

Since the menaces are not correctly placed, a simple squeeze against East in hearts and clubs is not possible. However, dummy has the ten-four of hearts. East, to guard his ace of hearts from being killed by a ruff, has to retain the ace-eight of hearts. This will enable South to reach the following ending:

(59)

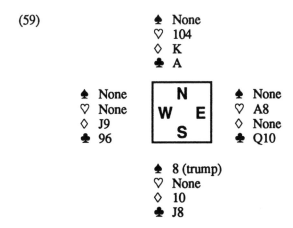

```
                    ♠ None
                    ♡ 104
                    ◊ K
                    ♣ A
   ♠ None      ┌─────────┐   ♠ None
   ♡ None      │ N       │   ♡ A8
   ◊ J9        │ W   E   │   ◊ None
   ♣ 96        │   S     │   ♣ Q10
              └─────────┘
                    ♠ 8 (trump)
                    ♡ None
                    ◊ 10
                    ♣ J8
```

Dummy's five of clubs has been discarded. South now leads the ten of diamonds to dummy's king, and East is squeezed. If he discards the small heart, dummy's four of hearts is led and ruffed with South's eight of trumps, dropping the ace and setting up North's ten of hearts as a winner. The ace of clubs is the re-entry to dummy to cash the established ten of hearts. If East discards the ten of clubs, North's ace of clubs drops East's queen, and South's jack becomes a winner. South still has a trump as the entry to cash the jack of clubs.

This is the first basic form of the single ruffing squeeze. These are the requirements:

North has a two-card ruffing menace against East as well as a squeeze-card (the king of diamonds); South has a trump; and there is a split two-card menace against East with the menace card (the jack of clubs) in the South hand and the master card (the ace of clubs) in the North hand.

If these conditions are satisfied, the North hand can be entered twice after the squeeze-card is played: once to lead the small heart from North for South to ruff, and a second time to cash the established ten of hearts. South's trump may also be used as an entry to the South hand to cash the jack of clubs if East chooses to discard the ten of clubs on the lead of the squeeze-card.

As the squeeze-card (the king of diamonds) is in the North hand, the lead is with North after the squeeze-card is played, so the squeeze-card is itself the first entry to the North hand.

The squeeze-card can be transferred to the South hand. In this case, the split two-card menace must be increased in length, i.e. an additional master card must be added to the club suit in the North hand so that the North hand can be entered twice in that suit.

For example, in the above hand, if, at trick four, West leads another diamond instead of the three of clubs, then dummy wins with the king of diamonds. The play proceeds as before. Since dummy has two entries in the club suit, the declarer can play the hand to the following five-card ending:

(60)

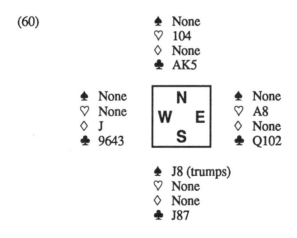

```
                    ♠ None
                    ♡ 104
                    ◇ None
                    ♣ AK5

    ♠ None        ┌─────────┐    ♠ None
    ♡ None        │    N    │    ♡ A8
    ◇ J           │  W   E  │    ◇ None
    ♣ 9643        │    S    │    ♣ Q102
                  └─────────┘
                    ♠ J8 (trumps)
                    ♡ None
                    ◇ None
                    ♣ J87
```

South leads the squeeze-card, the jack of spades, North throws the five of clubs, and East is ruffing-squeezed. If East discards the eight of hearts, dummy is entered with a club and the four of hearts led and ruffed, and North's cards are both winners. If East discards a club, then North's ace-king of clubs are played, dropping East's queen. The trump and the jack of clubs in the South hand win the last two tricks.

The situations in (59) and (60) are both automatic single ruffing squeezes against either opponents. However, when the East and West hands in (60) are interchanged, West will be subjected to a positional simple squeeze if South plays out the two trumps. These single ruffing squeezes are therefore of value only against the opponent to the left of the ruffing menace.

In the situation in diagram (60), the effect will be the same if the squeeze-card is in the diamond suit instead of being a trump. This enables another end position to exist:

(61)

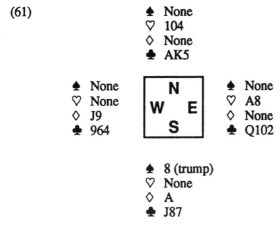

```
              ♠ None
              ♡ 104
              ◊ None
              ♣ AK5

  ♠ None      ┌─────────┐   ♠ None
  ♡ None      │   N     │   ♡ A8
  ◊ J9        │ W   E   │   ◊ None
  ♣ 964       │   S     │   ♣ Q102
              └─────────┘
              ♠ 8 (trump)
              ♡ None
              ◊ A
              ♣ J87
```

On the lead of the ace of diamonds, North discards the five of clubs and East is ruffing-squeezed. Like (59) and (60), this is also an automatic ruffing-squeeze situation.

Considering the above four-spade contract again, if West's trick-four diamond lead is won with dummy's king, the declarer can play the hand out to reach the same ending as in diagram (61).

The full deal is as follows:

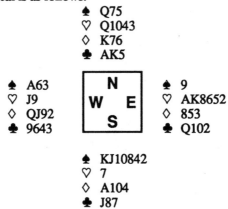

      ♠ Q75
      ♡ Q1043
      ◇ K76
      ♣ AK5

♠ A63   ♠ 9
♡ J9   ♡ AK8652
◇ QJ92   ◇ 853
♣ 9643   ♣ Q102

      ♠ KJ10842
      ♡ 7
      ◇ A104
      ♣ J87

In the single-ruffing-squeeze situation in diagram (60), if there is a master card in the suit of the ruffing menace, thus providing an entry to the North hand, one of the top winners in the club suit can be played at an earlier stage.

The result will be a new single ruffing squeeze. The following hand may lead to such an ending.

East-West game; Dealer West

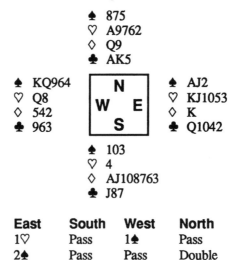

      ♠ 875
      ♡ A9762
      ◇ Q9
      ♣ AK5

♠ KQ964   ♠ AJ2
♡ Q8   ♡ KJ1053
◇ 542   ◇ K
♣ 963   ♣ Q1042

      ♠ 103
      ♡ 4
      ◇ AJ108763
      ♣ J87

East	South	West	North
1♡	Pass	1♠	Pass
2♠	Pass	Pass	Double
3♠	5◇	All Pass	

West takes the first two tricks with the king and queen of spades, then switches to a club, dummy's king winning.

The declarer plays the queen of diamonds intending to run it, but the king appears. Declarer plays the ace and four more rounds, leaving this position:

(62)

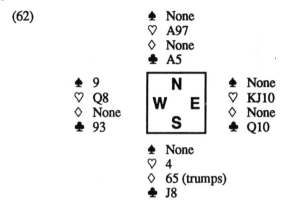

```
                    ♠ None
                    ♡ A97
                    ◇ None
                    ♣ A5
    ♠ 9           ┌─────────┐    ♠ None
    ♡ Q8          │    N    │    ♡ KJ10
    ◇ None        │ W     E │    ◇ None
    ♣ 93          │    S    │    ♣ Q10
                  └─────────┘
                    ♠ None
                    ♡ 4
                    ◇ 65 (trumps)
                    ♣ J8
```

South leads the six of diamonds, North discards the five of clubs and East is ruffing-squeezed. If East throws a heart, the ace of hearts is played and a heart led and ruffed, setting up a heart winner in dummy. If East discards the ten of clubs, South's jack of clubs can be established.

In this situation, one of the two entries in the North hand necessary for a ruffing squeeze is provided in the ruffing-menace suit itself. The other is in the suit of the single menace.

Of course, the squeeze-card may be in the fourth suit (i.e. spades) instead of being in the trump suit. This gives another situation:

(63)

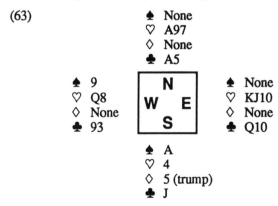

```
                    ♠ None
                    ♡ A97
                    ◇ None
                    ♣ A5
    ♠ 9           ┌─────────┐    ♠ None
    ♡ Q8          │    N    │    ♡ KJ10
    ◇ None        │ W     E │    ◇ None
    ♣ 93          │    S    │    ♣ Q10
                  └─────────┘
                    ♠ A
                    ♡ 4
                    ◇ 5 (trump)
                    ♣ J
```

On the lead of the ace of spades, North discards the five of clubs and East is ruffing-squeezed.

In the five-diamond example hand, if West leads a heart at trick three, the declarer can make the contract by playing to reach an end position similar to that in (60).

There is a true positional ruffing squeeze against West which is shown in the following diagram.

(64)

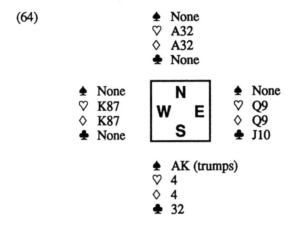

This is a six-card ending and South is on lead.

North has two three-card ruffing menaces against West, each containing a master card. The two master cards are at the same time two entries to the North hand.

South leads a trump card, and West has to find a discard. If West discards a heart, South can ruff a heart with the last trump card to set up a new winner in hearts. If West discards a diamond, South can likewise set up a diamond winner.

Note that in this situation South has four winners out of six cards. The last trick will be lost to East-West after the squeeze gains a trick for South.

This is illustrated in the following hand:

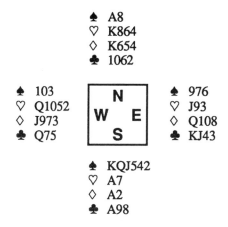

```
              ♠ A8
              ♡ K864
              ◊ K654
              ♣ 1062

♠ 103          ┌─────────┐          ♠ 976
♡ Q1052        │    N    │          ♡ J93
◊ J973         │ W     E │          ◊ Q108
♣ Q75          │    S    │          ♣ KJ43
               └─────────┘
              ♠ KQJ542
              ♡ A7
              ◊ A2
              ♣ A98
```

The contract is six spades by South and the opening lead is a spade. The declarer wins four trump tricks and cashes the three aces in the side suits, leaving this situation:

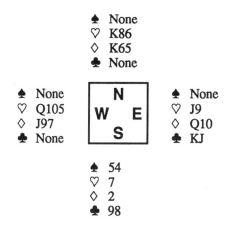

```
              ♠ None
              ♡ K86
              ◊ K65
              ♣ None

♠ None         ┌─────────┐          ♠ None
♡ Q105         │    N    │          ♡ J9
◊ J97          │ W     E │          ◊ Q10
♣ None         │    S    │          ♣ KJ
               └─────────┘
              ♠ 54
              ♡ 7
              ◊ 2
              ♣ 98
```

On the lead of the five of spades, West is subjected to a positional ruffing squeeze. The position is the same as in diagram (64). West, who has to retain the length in both his red suits, has been forced to discard all his clubs.

In the situation in diagram (64), the squeeze-card may be in the club suit. In this event another ending can be set up:

(65)

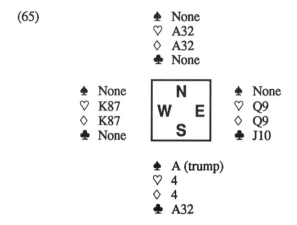

On the lead of the ace of clubs, West is ruffing-squeezed.

In the above example hand, if the declarer cashes the penultimate trump before the ace of clubs, the squeeze situation would be the same as in diagram (65).

6.2 Double ruffing squeezes

In a double ruffing squeeze there are two double menaces: one is a split two-card double menace; the other is a double ruffing menace.

This is the first basic situation:

(66)

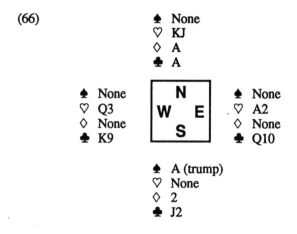

The heart suit in the North-South hands is a double ruffing menace and the club suit a split two-card double menace. On the lead of the ace of diamonds both opponents are squeezed simultaneously. If both opponents discard in clubs, the ace of clubs is played and the South hand is entered with a heart ruff to make the established jack of clubs. If West discards the three of hearts, the king of hearts is led. East has to cover, South ruffs, and North's jack becomes a winner. If East discards the two of hearts, the jack of hearts is led. East has to play his singleton ace, which South ruffs, and North's king of hearts is established. The ace of clubs is the entry to the North hand to cash the established heart winner.

This is the situation corresponding to the single-ruffing-squeeze position in (59).

If the squeeze-card is in the South hand, an additional master card must be added in the split-double-menace suit in the North hand. In this event the squeeze-card may be either in the trump suit or in the fourth suit. The situations corresponding to the single-ruffing-squeeze situations in (60) and (61) are:

(67)

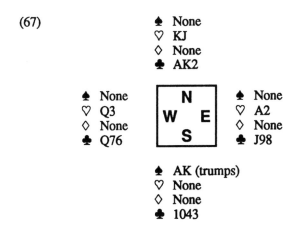

    ♠ None
    ♡ KJ
    ◇ None
    ♣ AK2

♠ None   ♠ None
♡ Q3   ♡ A2
◇ None   ◇ None
♣ Q76   ♣ J98

    ♠ AK (trumps)
    ♡ None
    ◇ None
    ♣ 1043

(68)

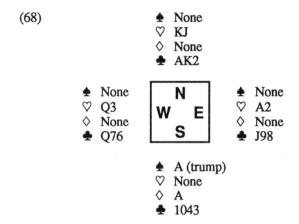

```
                   ♠ None
                   ♡ KJ
                   ◊ None
                   ♣ AK2

♠ None         ┌──────────┐         ♠ None
♡ Q3           │    N     │         ♡ A2
◊ None         │ W     E  │         ◊ None
♣ Q76          │    S     │         ♣ J98
               └──────────┘
                   ♠ A (trump)
                   ♡ None
                   ◊ A
                   ♣ 1043
```

On the lead of the ace of spades in (67) or ace of diamonds in (68) both opponents are squeezed simultaneously in the two-card double-ruffing-menace suit and the split three-card double-menace suit.

The three-card double ruffing menace with a master card in the suit described in Chapter 1 can be used to set up a double-ruffing-squeeze situation as shown in the next diagram:

(69)

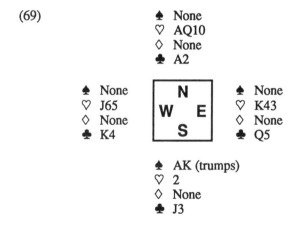

```
                   ♠ None
                   ♡ AQ10
                   ◊ None
                   ♣ A2

♠ None         ┌──────────┐         ♠ None
♡ J65          │    N     │         ♡ K43
◊ None         │ W     E  │         ◊ None
♣ K4           │    S     │         ♣ Q5
               └──────────┘
                   ♠ AK (trumps)
                   ♡ 2
                   ◊ None
                   ♣ J3
```

On the lead of the ace of spades, North discards the two of clubs, and West and East are squeezed simultaneously. If both opponents discard in clubs, the jack of clubs can be established. If either opponent discards a heart, an extra trick can be set up in hearts.

116

A similar situation is set up if the squeeze-card is in the diamond suit:

(70)

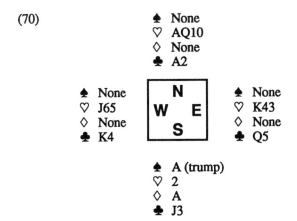

```
              ♠  None
              ♡  AQ10
              ◇  None
              ♣  A2
  ♠  None    ┌─────────┐   ♠  None
  ♡  J65     │    N    │   ♡  K43
  ◇  None    │  W   E  │   ◇  None
  ♣  K4      │    S    │   ♣  Q5
             └─────────┘
              ♠  A (trump)
              ♡  2
              ◇  A
              ♣  J3
```

The lead of the ace of diamonds, on which North lets go of the two of clubs, squeezes West and East simultaneously.

The following hand is an example of a double ruffing squeeze.

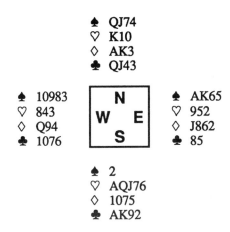

```
              ♠  QJ74
              ♡  K10
              ◇  AK3
              ♣  QJ43
  ♠  10983   ┌─────────┐   ♠  AK65
  ♡  843     │    N    │   ♡  952
  ◇  Q94     │  W   E  │   ◇  J862
  ♣  1076    │    S    │   ♣  85
             └─────────┘
              ♠  2
              ♡  AQJ76
              ◇  1075
              ♣  AK92
```

The contract is six hearts by South. West leads the ten of spades, dummy covers with the jack, and East wins with the king. A heart is returned. The declarer wins two heart tricks in dummy, comes to the South hand with a club, and draws a third round of trumps, North discarding a club. After the queen and jack of clubs are cashed, a spade is led and ruffed, to leave this ending:

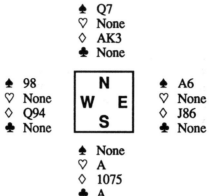

```
              ♠ Q7
              ♡ None
              ◊ AK3
              ♣ None

♠ 98         ┌─────────┐      ♠ A6
♡ None       │    N    │      ♡ None
◊ Q94        │ W     E │      ◊ J86
♣ None       │    S    │      ♣ None
             └─────────┘
              ♠ None
              ♡ A
              ◊ 1075
              ♣ A
```

The ace of clubs is now played, North discards the three of diamonds, and the opponents are caught simultaneously in a double ruffing squeeze. The end position is the same as in diagram (68).

6.3 Triple ruffing squeezes

A triple ruffing squeeze is a squeeze of an opponent in three suits in one of which he is ruffing-menaced.

A basic triple-ruffing-squeeze position can be set up by combining a single ruffing menace with two split two-card menaces against an opponent:

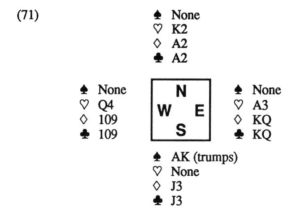

```
(71)          ♠ None
              ♡ K2
              ◊ A2
              ♣ A2

♠ None       ┌─────────┐      ♠ None
♡ Q4         │    N    │      ♡ A3
◊ 109        │ W     E │      ◊ KQ
♣ 109        │    S    │      ♣ KQ
             └─────────┘
              ♠ AK (trumps)
              ♡ None
              ◊ J3
              ♣ J3
```

South has four winners out of six cards. On the lead of the ace of spades, North discards the two of diamonds or the two of clubs and East is squeezed. If East discards the three of hearts, the North hand is entered with an ace and the two of hearts led and ruffed, setting up North's king of hearts as a winner. The other ace in the North hand is the entry to make it. If East discards in diamonds or clubs, the jack of the discarded suit in the South hand becomes a winner with the king of spades as the entry to cash it.

The two entries in the North hand can both be provided in one of the split menaces. In this case the other split menace may be replaced by a one-card menace. The situation becomes:

(72)

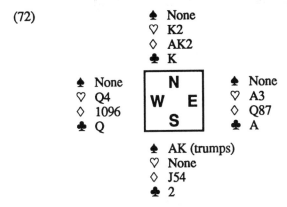

       ♠ None
       ♡ K2
       ◊ AK2
       ♣ K

♠ None   ♠ None
♡ Q4   ♡ A3
◊ 1096   ◊ Q87
♣ Q   ♣ A

        ♠ AK (trumps)
        ♡ None
        ◊ J54
        ♣ 2

The lead of the ace of spades subjects East to a triple ruffing squeeze. The one-card menace in the North hand may be transferred to the South hand. This enables another situation to exist:

(73)

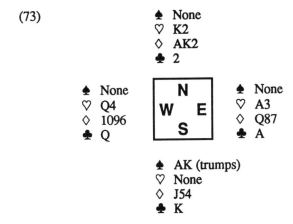

       ♠ None
       ♡ K2
       ◊ AK2
       ♣ 2

♠ None   ♠ None
♡ Q4   ♡ A3
◊ 1096   ◊ Q87
♣ Q   ♣ A

        ♠ AK (trumps)
        ♡ None
        ◊ J54
        ♣ K

This situation is easier to handle. On the lead of the ace of spades, North need not discard the two of diamonds—the two of clubs is an idle card that can be thrown freely. If East now chooses to discard the ace of clubs, he will be squeezed a second time.

The next hand is an example.

East-West game; Dealer East

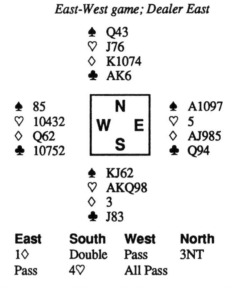

```
            ♠ Q43
            ♡ J76
            ◊ K1074
            ♣ AK6

♠ 85           N        ♠ A1097
♡ 10432    W       E    ♡ 5
◊ Q62          S        ◊ AJ985
♣ 10752                 ♣ Q94

            ♠ KJ62
            ♡ AKQ98
            ◊ 3
            ♣ J83
```

East	South	West	North
1◊	Double	Pass	3NT
Pass	4♡	All Pass	

West leads the queen of diamonds, dummy covers with the king, and East's ace wins. East leads the five of hearts. The declarer draws three rounds of trumps. On the fourth round the situation is as follows:

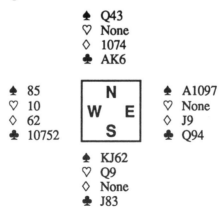

```
            ♠ Q43
            ♡ None
            ◊ 1074
            ♣ AK6

♠ 85           N        ♠ A1097
♡ 10        W       E   ♡ None
◊ 62           S        ◊ J9
♣ 10752                 ♣ Q94

            ♠ KJ62
            ♡ Q9
            ◊ None
            ♣ J83
```

On the lead of the queen of hearts, North lets go of a diamond (or a spade), and East is triple-ruffing-squeezed. This squeeze is a variation of the ending in (73). If East carelessly discards a spade, South can make eleven tricks. A further squeeze, this time a single ruffing squeeze, will operate against East at a later trick.

6.4 Unusual ruffing squeezes

A variation of an automatic single ruffing squeeze is illustrated in the following hand played by South in a contract of four spades.

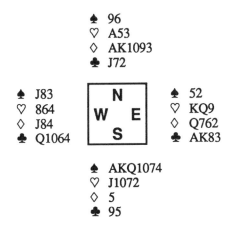

```
                ♠ 96
                ♡ A53
                ◊ AK1093
                ♣ J72

    ♠ J83       ┌─────────┐      ♠ 52
    ♡ 864       │    N    │      ♡ KQ9
    ◊ J84       │ W     E │      ◊ Q762
    ♣ Q1064     │    S    │      ♣ AK83
                └─────────┘

                ♠ AKQ1074
                ♡ J1072
                ◊ 5
                ♣ 95
```

The opening lead is the four of clubs. East wins the king and ace of clubs and leads another club, which South ruffs. South plays three rounds of trumps, dummy discarding a diamond.

There are nine top winners only. In order to set up a tenth winner, the declarer plays for an opponent to hold king-queen-small of hearts together with four or more diamonds.

At trick seven, the declarer accordingly leads the ten of spades, dummy discards a heart. If West or East holds originally four diamonds as well as king-queen-small in hearts, he is squeezed. In fact, the situation is now as follows:

(74)

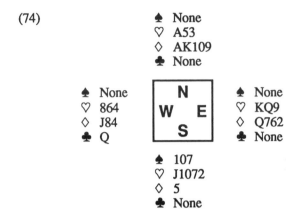

♠ None
♡ A53
◇ AK109
♣ None

♠ None
♡ 864
◇ J84
♣ Q

♠ None
♡ KQ9
◇ Q762
♣ None

♠ 107
♡ J1072
◇ 5
♣ None

The lead of the ten of spades squeezes East in hearts and diamonds. If East discards a heart, the ace of hearts is played and the small heart led from dummy. East wins a heart trick, but North-South win all the remaining four tricks. If East discards a diamond, the ace and king of diamonds are cashed and another diamond led and ruffed, establishing a diamond winner for North-South.

Another rare ruffing-squeeze ending can be reached in the following hand.

North-South game; Dealer South

♠ AQ8
♡ A932
◇ K3
♣ K762

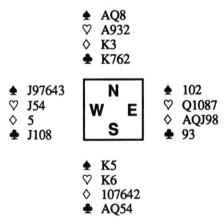

♠ J97643
♡ J54
◇ 5
♣ J108

♠ 102
♡ Q1087
◇ AQJ98
♣ 93

♠ K5
♡ K6
◇ 107642
♣ AQ54

The final contract is five clubs by South, although three no-trumps is probably the best contract.

West leads the five of diamonds, dummy plays low, East wins with the jack and leads a club, won by South's queen. South leads a diamond to North's king and East's ace, West discards a spade. East leads another club to South's ace. The declarer plays the king of clubs and the king and queen of spades. At trick eight, the situation is as follows:

(75)

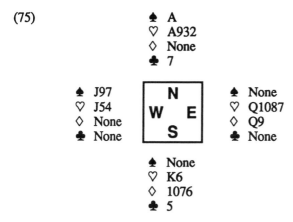

```
              ♠  A
              ♡  A932
              ◇  None
              ♣  7

 ♠  J97       ┌─────────┐    ♠  None
 ♡  J54       │ N       │    ♡  Q1087
 ◇  None      │ W     E │    ◇  Q9
 ♣  None      │   S     │    ♣  None
              └─────────┘
              ♠  None
              ♡  K6
              ◇  1076
              ♣  5
```

In this six-card ending South can win five tricks by cross-ruffing. However, the ace of spades is now played, South discards a diamond and East is squeezed. The hearts and diamonds in the North-South hands are two ruffing menaces against East. If East discards a heart, the king and ace of hearts are played and another heart led and ruffed, making good the last heart in the North hand. If East discards a diamond, the king of hearts is played and a diamond led and ruffed in dummy. The last diamond in the South hand becomes a winner.

This is an automatic-ruffing-squeeze situation. West will be squeezed if he holds East's cards.

Chapter 7

Guard Squeezes

7.1 Single guard squeezes

A single guard squeeze is a squeeze of one opponent in three suits in one of which he is guard-menaced.

(76)

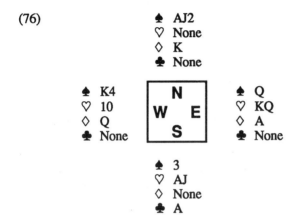

	♠ AJ2
	♡ None
	◇ K
	♣ None

The combination of North's ace-jack and South's three of spades is a guard menace against East. If East discards his lone queen of spades, South can lead the three of spades and finesse North's jack if West plays low.

In this four-card ending, South leads the ace of clubs, North throws the two of spades, and East is squeezed in three suits. He cannot discard the queen of spades. If he discards a heart, South wins two heart tricks. If he discards the ace of diamonds, South cashes the ace of hearts and then wins the last two tricks with North's ace of spades and king of diamonds.

It must be noted that South should not cash the ace of hearts before leading the ace of clubs. Otherwise North will have no idle card to discard on the lead of the ace of clubs and the squeeze fails.

This is a basic guard squeeze against East. To have a situation where the opponent to the left of the squeeze-card is guard-squeezed, the guard menace should be split and of three-card length.

(77)

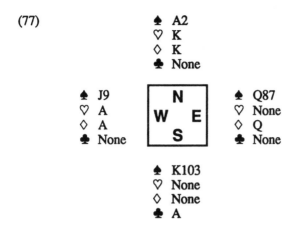

```
            ♠ A2
            ♡ K
            ◇ K
            ♣ None

♠ J9        ┌─────────┐    ♠ Q87
♡ A         │    N    │    ♡ None
◇ A         │ W     E │    ◇ Q
♣ None      │    S    │    ♣ None
            └─────────┘
            ♠ K103
            ♡ None
            ◇ None
            ♣ A
```

South leads the ace of clubs and West is subjected to a guard squeeze. The combination of the North-South spades is a split three-card guard menace against West. If West discards the nine of spades, South leads the three of spades to West's jack and North's ace. North then leads the two of spades and takes the finesse against East's queen. If West discards in hearts or diamonds, North wins an extra trick in the discarded suit.

Let us study the following hand played by South in a contract of six hearts.

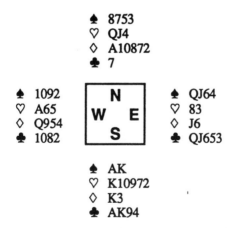

```
            ♠ 8753
            ♡ QJ4
            ◇ A10872
            ♣ 7

♠ 1092      ┌─────────┐    ♠ QJ64
♡ A65       │    N    │    ♡ 83
◇ Q954      │ W     E │    ◇ J6
♣ 1082      │    S    │    ♣ QJ653
            └─────────┘
            ♠ AK
            ♡ K10972
            ◇ K3
            ♣ AK94
```

West leads the ace and another heart to dummy's jack. This defensive play prevents the declarer from ruffing two clubs in dummy and making an easy slam. However, there are still several possibilities.

The first possibility is a three-three break in diamonds.

The second line of play is to ruff a club in dummy and a spade in the South hand, and then play for a simple squeeze against West in spades and diamonds. This play requires West to have queen-jack-small or at least four cards in diamonds.

The third line of play is to ruff a club and a spade, and then play for a double squeeze on the assumption that East guards clubs and West guards spades, the ace-ten of diamonds being a two-card double menace. The end position would be the same as in diagram (15).

The fourth line of play is to ruff a club and a spade, and then play for an automatic simple squeeze in diamonds and clubs. This play requires that the opponent who guards the club suit has also queen-jack-small or at least four cards in diamonds.

A simple squeeze in spades and clubs does not exist, since there are no entry cards in the suits of the two menaces.

In fact, a careful analysis will show that, if the second or fourth line of play works, the third line of play also works. That is to say, the third line of play takes care of the possibilities of both the second and the fourth cases. At trick 11, the North-South cards are:

♠ 8
♡ None
♦ A10
♣ None

♠ None
♡ K
♦ 3
♣ 9

South leads the king of hearts.

If West has the master spade, East has the master club, and both opponents guard the diamond suit, the third line of play succeeds.

If West has the only stoppers in both spades and diamonds, the above play also succeeds. Therefore the third line of play takes into account the second line of play.

If East or West has the only stoppers in both diamonds and clubs, the above play also succeeds. Therefore the third line of play takes into account the fourth line of play as well.

But unfortunately the second, third and fourth lines of play all fail. The spade and club suits are stopped by East, while West holds originally four diamonds to the queen.

Now, can it be true that six hearts is an impossible contract?

Suppose we have not cashed both club winners, but have preserved the king of clubs. Instead of the above three-card ending, we play the hand to a four-card ending, then the situation will be quite different:

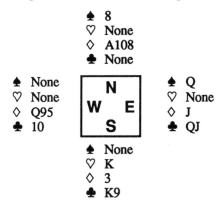

```
              ♠  8
              ♡  None
              ◇  A108
              ♣  None
  ♠  None      ┌─────────┐   ♠  Q
  ♡  None      │    N    │   ♡  None
  ◇  Q95       │  W   E  │   ◇  J
  ♣  10        │    S    │   ♣  QJ
              └─────────┘
              ♠  None
              ♡  K
              ◇  3
              ♣  K9
```

South leads the king of hearts, North discards the eight of diamonds, and East is guard-squeezed. If he discards the jack of diamonds, South can cash the king of clubs and then take a finesse in diamonds. If East discards in the spade or club suit, South wins an extra trick in the discarded suit. This is the same guard-squeeze situation as in diagram (76).

This line of play not only succeeds for the actual deal given above, but also takes care of the possibilities of the third and hence the second and the fourth cases in our analysis. We leave it to the readers to check this.

In diagram (77), either of the two ordinary one-card menaces may be increased in length. In this case, the other one-card menace may be transferred to the South hand. For example, if the one-card heart menace against West is replaced by a two-card menace, the one-card diamond menace may be in the South hand:

(78)

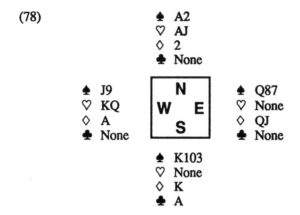

```
              ♠  A2
              ♡  AJ
              ◊  2
              ♣  None

♠  J9         ┌─────────┐      ♠  Q87
♡  KQ         │    N    │      ♡  None
◊  A          │  W   E  │      ◊  QJ
♣  None       │    S    │      ♣  None
              └─────────┘
              ♠  K103
              ♡  None
              ◊  K
              ♣  A
```

On the lead of the ace of clubs West is single-guard-squeezed.

7.2   A suicide guard squeeze

Consider the following hand.

North-South game; Dealer South

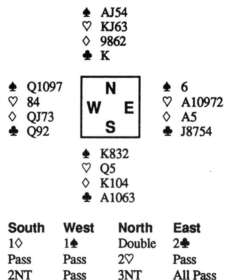

```
              ♠  AJ54
              ♡  KJ63
              ◊  9862
              ♣  K

♠  Q1097      ┌─────────┐      ♠  6
♡  84         │    N    │      ♡  A10972
◊  QJ73       │  W   E  │      ◊  A5
♣  Q92        │    S    │      ♣  J8754
              └─────────┘
              ♠  K832
              ♡  Q5
              ◊  K104
              ♣  A1063
```

South	West	North	East
1◊	1♠	Double	2♣
Pass	Pass	2♡	Pass
2NT	Pass	3NT	All Pass

West leads the three of diamonds, East wins with the ace and returns the five, South's king winning. South leads the two of spades, dummy finesses the jack. A small heart is led from dummy and South wins with the queen. At trick five, South leads the five of hearts and dummy's jack goes to East's ace. East returns the ten of hearts to dummy's king, South discarding a spade. The king of clubs is cashed. At trick eight, dummy's last heart is led and won by East. The six-card ending is as follows:

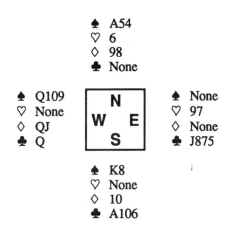

At this eighth trick, South discards the six of clubs and West is in trouble. Suppose West discards the jack of diamonds. If East wins another trick with the nine of hearts, South and North both discard a diamond, but West is in further difficulties. A spade or diamond discard concedes an immediate trick to South, and a club discard enables South to finesse the ten of clubs when East leads a club at the next trick.

This is an example of a guard squeeze against West. But here the squeeze-card is the nine of hearts led by East. It is not a card led by South. Moreover, North is now void in clubs, and it is East who leads a club at trick ten. The situation is in fact a suicide guard squeeze.

Returning to the six-card ending above, North leads the six of hearts to East's seven. West is subjected to a guard squeeze and the jack of diamonds is discarded. A diamond winner can now be set up in the North hand. Suppose that East leads a club instead of the nine of hearts at trick nine, then South wins this trick with the ace of clubs, on which North lets go of a spade, and plays the ten of diamonds. North-South win the last three tricks with the ace-king of spades and the nine of diamonds. If West discards the queen of clubs at trick eight, and East leads a club at trick nine, South can finesse the ten of clubs. Therefore, the above six-card ending is a guard squeeze to which there is no defence. North-South have three winners out of the six remaining cards. An additional trick can be set up for North-South by the squeeze. It is a suicide squeeze combining a guard squeeze with a trick-establishing play.

7.3 Non-simultaneous double guard squeezes

In the single-guard-squeeze situations in diagrams (76), (77) and (78), one of the opponents is guard-squeezed: he is guard-menaced in the spade suit, and single-menaced in hearts and diamonds. The other opponent has no stoppers except in the suit of the guard menace. If the latter holds a stopper in a suit other than that of the guard menace, it is possible that he will be subjected to a simple squeeze in two suits, since the guard menace is itself a double menace against both opponents.

The combination of a guard squeeze against one opponent and a simple squeeze against his partner is called a double guard squeeze.

The first situation is this:

(79)

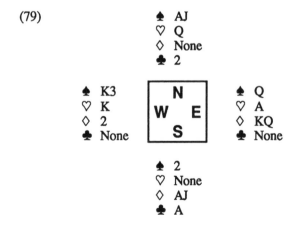

The spade combination in the North-South hands is a guard menace against East, North's queen of hearts is a one-card double menace, and South's ace-jack of diamonds is a two-card menace against East. On the lead of the ace of clubs, West discards the two of diamonds and East is guard-squeezed.

The discard of the queen of spades enables South to take a finesse in spades, and the discard of a diamond sets up South's jack of diamonds. East is forced to part with the ace of hearts. At the next trick, the ace of diamonds is led, squeezing West in spades and hearts.

This is a non-simultaneous double guard squeeze. East is guard-squeezed on the lead of the ace of clubs, and West is simple-squeezed at the next trick.

This is a symmetrical four-card ending:

(80)

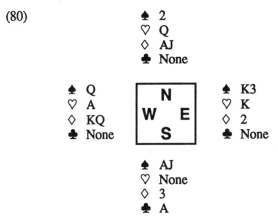

```
              ♠ 2
              ♡ Q
              ◊ AJ
              ♣ None

♠ Q                          ♠ K3
♡ A        N                 ♡ K
◊ KQ     W   E               ◊ 2
♣ None     S                 ♣ None

              ♠ AJ
              ♡ None
              ◊ 3
              ♣ A
```

Now the North-South spade combination is a guard menace against West. On the lead of the ace of clubs, West is guard-squeezed and has to let go of the ace of hearts. North discards the now useless jack of diamonds and, at the next trick, the ace of diamonds squeezes East in spades and hearts.

The following hand is an example.

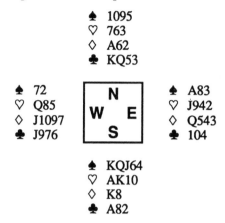

Against South's six no-trump contract, West leads the jack of diamonds, which is won with South's king. Spades are led and when East gets in with the ace he leads another diamond to the eight, nine and ace. The declarer plays the queen and ace of clubs, the king of hearts, and all but one of the spades, West discarding a heart on the penultimate spade. This is the position:

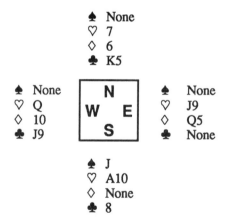

On the lead of the jack of spades, West is guard-squeezed. If he discards the queen of hearts, a finesse can be taken against East's jack of hearts. If he diacards a club, North's five of clubs is established. And if he discards the ten of diamonds, North lets go of the five of clubs, and East will be squeezed in hearts and diamonds on the lead of the king of clubs. The situation is the same as in diagram (80).

Observe that if West discards two diamonds on the third and fourth rounds of spades, the declarer can play the hand to a non-simultaneous double-squeeze ending as in diagram (17).

7.4 Simultaneous double guard squeezes

If we replace the one-card double menace in diagram (79) by a two-card double menace and the two-card menace against East by a one-card menace against East, we arrive at the following situation:

(81)

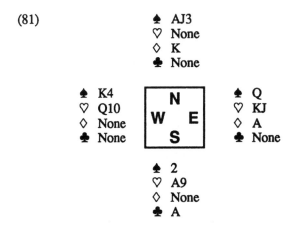

♠ AJ3
♥ None
♦ K
♣ None

♠ K4   ♠ Q
♥ Q10   ♥ KJ
♦ None   ♦ A
♣ None   ♣ None

♠ 2
♥ A9
♦ None
♣ A

On the lead of the ace of clubs, North discards the three of spades and the opponents are squeezed simultaneously. West is forced to discard a heart. If East discards the queen of spades, a finesse can be taken against West's king of spades. If East discards a heart, South wins two heart tricks. And if East discards the ace of diamonds, South wins a heart and North a spade and a diamond.

This is a basic end position of the simultaneous double guard squeeze with the guard squeeze against the opponent to the right of the squeeze-card. Since the squeeze is simultaneous, North need not have a small card in the heart suit. And if North has a small heart, the situation becomes that of the non-simultaneous double squeeze in diagram (17); the guard menace then serves merely as an ordinary two-card menace against West.

To obtain a basic simultaneous double guard squeeze with the squeeze acting on the opponent to the left of the squeeze-card, we replace the two-card guard menace in diagram (80) by a split three-card guard menace and the two-card menace against West by a one-card menace against West:[*]

(82)

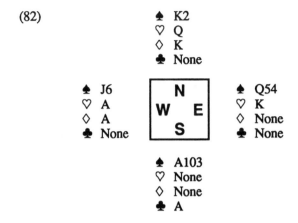

```
              ♠ K2
              ♡ Q
              ◊ K
              ♣ None

  ♠ J6       ┌─────────┐   ♠ Q54
  ♡ A        │    N    │   ♡ K
  ◊ A        │ W     E │   ◊ None
  ♣ None     │    S    │   ♣ None
             └─────────┘

              ♠ A103
              ♡ None
              ◊ None
              ♣ A
```

On the lead of the ace of clubs, West obviously cannot discard the ace of diamonds. If he discards a spade, the three of spades is led to North's king and a finesse taken against East's queen. If he discards the ace of hearts, North lets go of the king of diamonds, and East is simple-squeezed in spades and hearts.

The requirements of this double guard squeeze may be stated as follows: a split three-card guard menace with the three-card part in the same hand as the squeeze-card; a one-card menace against the opponent to the left of the squeeze-card and a one-card double menace opposite the squeeze-card.

The one-card double menace in (82) may be replaced by a longer menace. In this event the one-card menace against the opponent to the left of the squeeze-card may be in either hand:

[*] *Bridge Magazine*, September 1952.

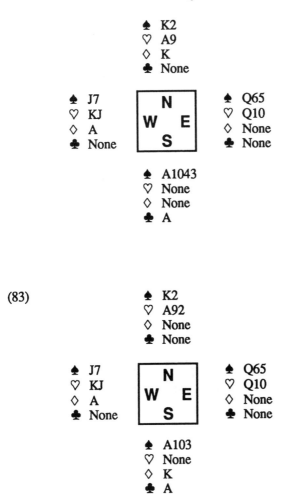

(83)

The one-card menace against the opponent to the left of the squeeze-card may also be replaced by a longer menace, and when this is the case the one-card double menace may be in either hand:

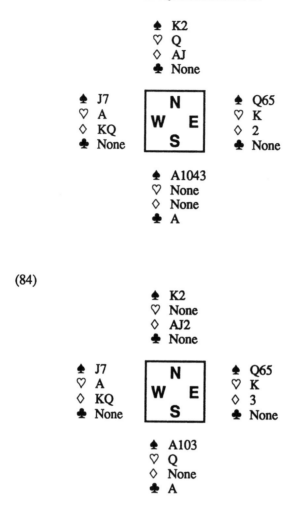

(84)

If the one-card double menace is increased in length, the squeeze is still simultaneous, whereas if the one-card menace against the opponent to the left of the squeeze-card is increased in length the squeeze becomes non-simultaneous: the opponent subjected to the guard squeeze will be squeezed first, and the simple squeeze against his partner will operate at a later trick.

The following hand is an example.

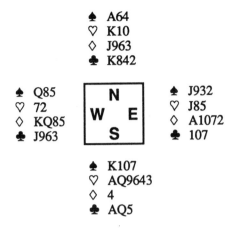

♠ A64
♡ K10
◊ J963
♣ K842

♠ Q85   ♠ J932
♡ 72   ♡ J85
◊ KQ85   ◊ A1072
♣ J963   ♣ 107

♠ K107
♡ AQ9643
◊ 4
♣ AQ5

The contract is six hearts by South. West wins the first trick with the king of diamonds. At trick two, the five of diamonds is led and ruffed by South. The declarer can play the hand to the following ending if West discards a spade on South's long hearts:

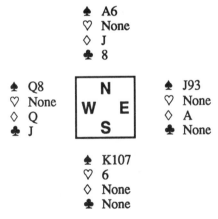

♠ A6
♡ None
◊ J
♣ 8

♠ Q8   ♠ J93
♡ None   ♡ None
◊ Q   ◊ A
♣ J   ♣ None

♠ K107
♡ 6
◊ None
♣ None

The lead of the six of hearts squeezes both opponents simultaneously. The situation is the same as in diagram (82).

If West holds on to his spades, the declarer can play the hand to the following ordinary double-squeeze situation:

137

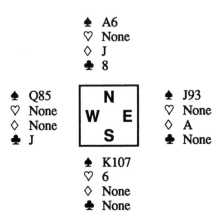

```
         ♠ A6
         ♡ None
         ◊ J
         ♣ 8
♠ Q85    ┌─────┐   ♠ J93
♡ None   │  N  │   ♡ None
◊ None   │ W E │   ◊ A
♣ J      │  S  │   ♣ None
         └─────┘
         ♠ K107
         ♡ 6
         ◊ None
         ♣ None
```

This is the simultaneous-double-squeeze situation in diagram (16).

7.5 Unusual double guard squeezes

In the double-guard-squeeze situation in (80), the ordinary one-card double menace may be replaced by a pick-up double menace. In this event a trick is lost after the guard squeeze takes place.

(85)

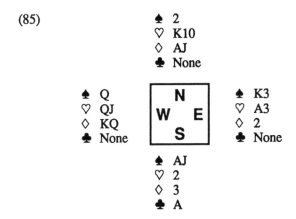

```
         ♠ 2
         ♡ K10
         ◊ AJ
         ♣ None
♠ Q      ┌─────┐   ♠ K3
♡ QJ     │  N  │   ♡ A3
◊ KQ     │ W E │   ◊ 2
♣ None   │  S  │   ♣ None
         └─────┘
         ♠ AJ
         ♡ 2
         ◊ 3
         ♣ A
```

The spade suit in the North-South hands is a guard menace against West, the heart suit is a pick-up double menace, and the diamond suit is a two-card menace against West.

138

On the lead of the ace of clubs, West is guard-squeezed and has to part with a heart. North and East both discard in diamonds. The ten of hearts can then be established with the ace of diamonds as the entry to make it.

This is a double guard squeeze with the squeeze against the opponent to the left of the squeeze-card. A similar form of double guard squeeze, with the guard squeeze against the opponent to the right of the squeeze-card, can be constructed by introducing a split three-card guard menace to diagram (79), and replacing the one-card double menace by a pick-up double menace.

(86)

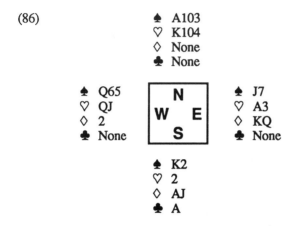

♠ A103
♥ K104
♦ None
♣ None

♠ Q65   ♠ J7
♥ QJ   ♥ A3
♦ 2   ♦ KQ
♣ None   ♣ None

♠ K2
♥ 2
♦ AJ
♣ A

On the lead of the ace of clubs, West discards the two of diamonds and North the four of hearts. East is squeezed and has to bare the ace of hearts. The king of hearts is then established by first conceding a trick to East's ace. South wins the last four tricks with the ace of diamonds, the king and ace of spades, and the king of hearts.

It must be noted that before leading the ace of clubs neither the king of spades nor the ace of diamonds can be cashed without damaging the squeeze. In the former case, East would lead the jack of spades when he is in with the ace of hearts, and a trick has to be conceded to West's queen of spades. In the latter case, if East is put into lead, he would immediately cash a diamond trick.

In the following hand, South is declarer at a contract of three no-trumps.

♠ 652
♡ K74
◇ K853
♣ A52

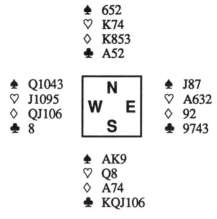

♠ Q1043   ♠ J87
♡ J1095   ♡ A632
◇ QJ106   ◇ 92
♣ 8   ♣ 9743

♠ AK9
♡ Q8
◇ A74
♣ KQJ106

West leads the queen of diamonds, which is allowed to hold. At trick two, the jack of hearts is led, South's queen winning. The declarer plays four rounds of clubs together with the ace of spades and ace of diamonds and the following position is reached:

♠ 6
♡ K7
◇ K8
♣ None

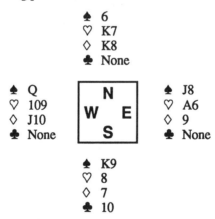

♠ Q   ♠ J8
♡ 109   ♡ A6
◇ J10   ◇ 9
♣ None   ♣ None

♠ K9
♡ 8
◇ 7
♣ 10

Two of West's spades have been discarded on South's long clubs. He cannot afford to discard in hearts, for otherwise North's seven of hearts can be established easily. The ten of clubs is now led and West is guard-squeezed.

This is the same situation as in diagram (85). The declarer eventually makes eleven tricks.

Chapter 8

Clash Squeezes*

A squeeze which contains a clash menace is called a clash squeeze. The following North-South cards form a clash menace against West:

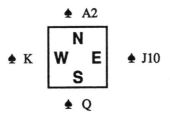

♠ A2

♠ K   N W E S   ♠ J10

♠ Q

West's king and South's queen will clash under North's ace. Yet, if entries are available, West cannot afford to discard the king, as it will enable North-South to make the queen and ace separately.

In the above diagram, if the East-West cards are interchanged the North-South combination is a clash menace against East.

To ensure the effectiveness of these clash menaces, it is necessary in almost all clash-squeeze situations that a side entry be kept in the North hand so that, should the king be discarded, the North hand can be entered to cash the ace after the lone queen has been made.

Exceptions to this do exist. There are cases in which a clash squeeze is combined with a trick-establishing or throw-in play, where no extra entry to the hand with the longer part of the clash menace is needed to effect the squeeze.

8.1 Single clash squeezes

A single clash squeeze is a squeeze of one opponent in three suits in one of which he is clash-menaced.

In view of the fact that a side entry should be kept to the hand with the longer part of the clash menace so that the clash squeeze may be successfully executed, there must be in the combined hands, as a clash squeeze begins to operate, at least a clash menace, a two-card menace, a

---

* The author's series of articles "All the Clash Squeezes" appeared in *Bridge Magazine*, July, August, October, November 1956; January, August, October 1957; August 1958; September 1959; May 1960; and August 1964.

one-card menace and a squeeze-card. Hence the minimum number of cards to be held in the combined hands is eight: three in the clash-menace suit, three in the two-card menace suit, one in the one-card menace suit and finally squeeze-card. Consequently, the opponent subjected to a single clash squeeze is required to hold a minimum of four cards, all of which must be busy.

The simplest form of single clash squeeze is shown in the following diagram:

(87)

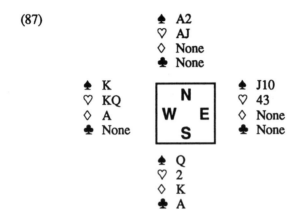

```
                    ♠  A2
                    ♡  AJ
                    ◊  None
                    ♣  None
    ♠  K          ┌─────────┐      ♠  J10
    ♡  KQ         │    N    │      ♡  43
    ◊  A          │ W     E │      ◊  None
    ♣  None       │    S    │      ♣  None
                  └─────────┘
                    ♠  Q
                    ♡  2
                    ◊  K
                    ♣  A
```

At no-trumps or with clubs as trumps the ace of clubs is led and West is clash-squeezed. The discard of the king of spades will enable South's queen and North's ace to be made separately, a heart discard sets up North's jack of hearts, and the discard of the ace of diamonds makes good South's king of diamonds. The combination of the cards renders the squeeze inescapable.

In diagram (87), each of the three menaces may be replaced by a longer menace of the same type without affecting the nature of the squeeze. If, for instance, the ordinary two-card menace is replaced by a three-card menace, the situation becomes:

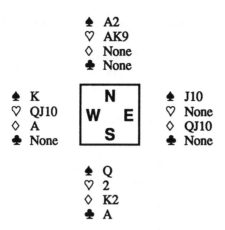

♠ A2
♡ AK9
◇ None
♣ None

♠ K　　♠ J10
♡ QJ10　♡ None
◇ A　　◇ QJ10
♣ None　♣ None

♠ Q
♡ 2
◇ K2
♣ A

Again, West is clash-squeezed on the lead of the ace of clubs.

The situation in diagram (87) is a positional squeeze. The squeeze fails if the West and East hands are interchanged. To have a situation where the single clash squeeze is automatic, we need only replace the one-card menace in diagram (87) with a two-card menace:

(88)

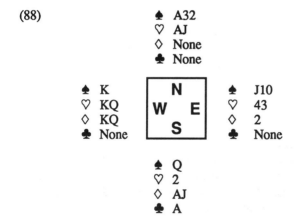

♠ A32
♡ AJ
◇ None
♣ None

♠ K　　♠ J10
♡ KQ　♡ 43
◇ KQ　◇ 2
♣ None　♣ None

♠ Q
♡ 2
◇ AJ
♣ A

On the lead of the ace of clubs, North discards the two of spades and West is clash-squeezed. This is an automatic single clash squeeze. The squeeze is equally effective if the West and East hands are interchanged.

It should be noted that the situations shown in diagrams (87) and (88) are not true clash squeezes. Both can be reduced to simple squeezes. In diagram (87), the ace of spades may be played at an earlier stage to leave a simple automatic squeeze. Similarly in diagram (88), if the ace of spades and ace of diamonds are both played earlier, the result is likewise a simple automatic squeeze. But often in a whole deal the lie of the cards is such that there is no opportunity to do the reduction. It is for this reason that these situations are given, serving as an introduction to the more essential and useful positions that will be treated subsequently.

We know that there are cases in which a squeeze may come into operation without requiring the "all-but-one" condition.

A single clash squeeze of this variety is shown in the following diagram.

(89)

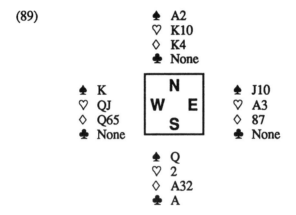

```
                    ♠ A2
                    ♡ K10
                    ◇ K4
                    ♣ None
      ♠ K        ┌─────────┐      ♠ J10
      ♡ QJ       │   N     │      ♡ A3
      ◇ Q65      │ W   E   │      ◇ 87
      ♣ None     │   S     │      ♣ None
                 └─────────┘
                    ♠ Q
                    ♡ 2
                    ◇ A32
                    ♣ A
```

The heart suit in the North-South hands is a pick-up double menace. South has four winners out of six cards.

To come to a fifth trick, the ace of clubs is played, squeezing West in three suits. He can neither discard in spades nor in diamonds, and if he throws a heart, North throws the two of spades. At the next trick, South leads the two of hearts on which North plays the king, losing to East's ace. Any return by East gives South the rest.

As it is, in this situation a trick is lost after the squeeze, which gains a trick for North-South.

A hand which may develop into such an end position is shown as follows:

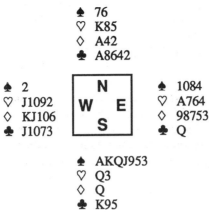

```
            ♠  76
            ♡  K85
            ◇  A42
            ♣  A8642

♠  2          N          ♠  1084
♡  J1092   W     E       ♡  A764
◇  KJ106                  ◇  98753
♣  J1073      S           ♣  Q

            ♠  AKQJ953
            ♡  Q3
            ◇  Q
            ♣  K95
```

Against South's six-spade contract West leads the jack of hearts on which North plays low. East ducks and South's queen wins the trick. The declarer counts only eleven tricks on top, yet he cannot afford to give away a trick to "rectify the count" without damaging the hand.

However, the ace of hearts seems to be with East, and if West happens to hold the ten-nine of hearts as well as the king of diamonds and long clubs, the contract can be made through a clash squeeze.

Six rounds of trumps are played, North discarding a diamond and three clubs. The position is:

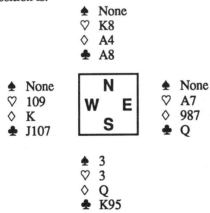

```
            ♠  None
            ♡  K8
            ◇  A4
            ♣  A8

♠  None       N          ♠  None
♡  109     W     E        ♡  A7
◇  K                      ◇  987
♣  J107       S           ♣  Q

            ♠  3
            ♡  3
            ◇  Q
            ♣  K95
```

Now the three of spades is played and West is single-clash-squeezed.

The situation in (89) is, strictly speaking, not a single clash squeeze, as East also guards the heart suit, a suit other than that of the clash menace. The situation can be reduced to a very important and interesting one, which will be discussed later.

8.2 *Non-simultaneous double clash squeezes*

A double clash squeeze is a combination of a clash squeeze against one opponent and a simple squeeze against the other. It can be a clash against the opponent to the left of the squeeze-card and a simple against his partner or vice versa.

We have already mentioned that a clash menace is also a double menace against both opponents. It follows that when the partner of the opponent subjected to a clash squeeze holds protection in a suit other than that of the clash menace, a double-clash-squeeze situation may possibly be formed.

We begin by considering the following ordinary double-squeeze situation.

```
            ♠ K
            ♡ 2
            ◇ AJ
            ♣ None

♠ None                      ♠ A
♡ K4                        ♡ Q5
◇ KQ                        ◇ 3
♣ None                      ♣ None

            ♠ None
            ♡ A3
            ◇ 2
            ♣ A
```

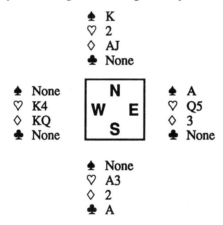

This is a non-simultaneous double squeeze. On the lead of the ace of clubs, West is forced to discard a heart. North throws the jack of diamonds and East the three of diamonds. At the next trick, the ace of diamonds squeezes East in spades and hearts.

It is easily seen that, if the one-card menace against East is replaced by a two-card menace, the squeeze fails, for West would then have an idle card to throw on the lead of the ace of clubs.

However, by introducing a clash menace against West we get a double-clash-squeeze situation:

(90)

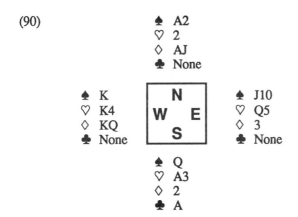

♠ A2
♥ 2
♦ AJ
♣ None

♠ K   ♠ J10
♥ K4   ♥ Q5
♦ KQ   ♦ 3
♣ None   ♣ None

♠ Q
♥ A3
♦ 2
♣ A

On the lead of the ace of clubs, West is clash-squeezed.

He cannot discard in spades or diamonds and so has to unguard the heart suit. North and East both discard in diamonds. The ace of diamonds is played and East is simple-squeezed in spades and hearts.

Admittedly the ace of spades, if played at an earlier stage, reduces the situation to that of the original ordinary double squeeze. But starting from this diagram we can arrive at several true forms of the non-simultaneous double clash squeeze.

The first basic situation is obtained by playing off the ace of hearts and increasing the length of the diamond suit in diagram (90).

(91)

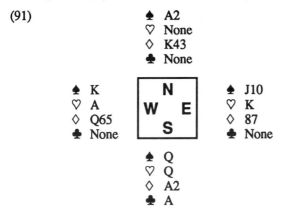

♠ A2
♥ None
♦ K43
♣ None

♠ K   ♠ J10
♥ A   ♥ K
♦ Q65   ♦ 87
♣ None   ♣ None

♠ Q
♥ Q
♦ A2
♣ A

The ace of clubs, is the squeeze-card. The spade suit is a clash menace against West, the queen of hearts is a one-card double menace, and the diamond suit is a split three-card menace against West. On the lead of the ace of clubs, West is clash-squeezed. If he discards the king of spades, the queen and ace will be made separately. If he throws a diamond, North-South will win three tricks in that suit. So he has to part with the ace of hearts. North throws a diamond. The king and ace of diamonds are played and, on the ace of diamonds, East is simple-squeezed in spades and hearts.

It should be noted that an earlier play of either the ace of spades or the ace of diamonds will damage the squeeze. In both cases West can safely throw the ace of hearts on the ace of clubs. East has no difficulty in his discarding.

In the following hand, South is the declarer at a contract of six no-trumps.

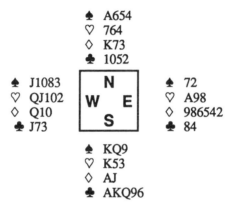

```
                    ♠ A654
                    ♡ 764
                    ◇ K73
                    ♣ 1052
    ♠ J1083      ┌─────────┐    ♠ 72
    ♡ QJ102      │   N     │    ♡ A98
    ◇ Q10        │ W   E   │    ◇ 986542
    ♣ J73        │   S     │    ♣ 84
                 └─────────┘
                    ♠ KQ9
                    ♡ K53
                    ◇ AJ
                    ♣ AKQ96
```

West leads the queen of hearts, East wins with the ace and returns the suit. South's king wins. The ace of diamonds is played and four rounds of clubs leave this position:

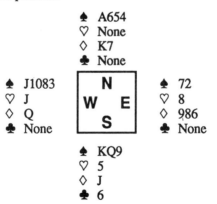

```
                    ♠ A654
                    ♡ None
                    ◇ K7
                    ♣ None
    ♠ J1083      ┌─────────┐    ♠ 72
    ♡ J          │   N     │    ♡ 8
    ◇ Q          │ W   E   │    ◇ 986
    ♣ None       │   S     │    ♣ None
                 └─────────┘
                    ♠ KQ9
                    ♡ 5
                    ◇ J
                    ♣ 6
```

On the lead of the six of clubs, West is clash-squeezed and has to discard the jack of hearts. North discards a spade. Three rounds of spades are played, ending in the declarer's hand. On the third round of spades, East is squeezed in hearts and diamonds.

In his book *Winning Defence*, John Brown used the following hand to illustrate a defensive technique against a declarer's squeeze play:

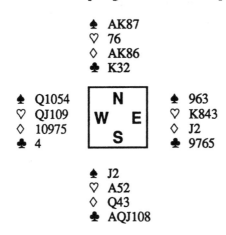

```
              ♠  AK87
              ♡  76
              ◊  AK86
              ♣  K32

  ♠  Q1054     N      ♠  963
  ♡  QJ109   W   E    ♡  K843
  ◊  10975     S      ◊  J2
  ♣  4                ♣  9765

              ♠  J2
              ♡  A52
              ◊  Q43
              ♣  AQJ108
```

The contract is six no-trumps by South, and West leads the queen of hearts, which South ducks. A heart is continued and South's ace wins.

It was pointed out that East should not discard a spade, otherwise the contract could be made through a simple squeeze of West in spades and diamonds.

In fact, this hand is an excellent example of a double clash squeeze. The king of diamonds, king of spades and four rounds of clubs are played. On the fourth round of clubs, West is forced to unguard hearts or to bare the queen of spades. In the former case, South makes his contract through an ordinary double squeeze (cash the ace-queen of diamonds and then play the last club); in the latter case, a double clash squeeze is successful:

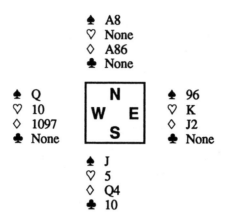

```
            ♠ A8
            ♡ None
            ◊ A86
            ♣ None
♠ Q        ┌─────────┐     ♠ 96
♡ 10       │    N    │     ♡ K
◊ 1097     │ W     E │     ◊ J2
♣ None     │    S    │     ♣ None
           └─────────┘
            ♠ J
            ♡ 5
            ◊ Q4
            ♣ 10
```

South leads the ten of clubs, the squeeze-card. The situation is exactly the same as in diagram (91).

A second form of non-simultaneous double clash squeeze is obtained if, in diagram (90), the two-card double menace is replaced by a one-card double menace and the two-card clash menace by a split three-card clash menace.

(92)

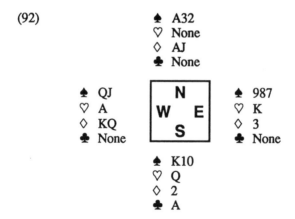

```
            ♠ A32
            ♡ None
            ◊ AJ
            ♣ None
♠ QJ       ┌─────────┐     ♠ 987
♡ A        │    N    │     ♡ K
◊ KQ       │ W     E │     ◊ 3
♣ None     │    S    │     ♣ None
           └─────────┘
            ♠ K10
            ♡ Q
            ◊ 2
            ♣ A
```

The spade combination in the North-South hands is a split three-card clash menace against West. If West discards a spade, the king, ten and ace of spades can be made in turn, so West is forced to unguard the heart suit on the lead of the ace of clubs. North discards the jack of diamonds. Now the ace of diamonds squeezes East in spades and hearts.

The hand on page (92) may also be used to illustrate diagram (92). In the same contract and with the same play to the first two tricks, the following end position can easily be arrived at:

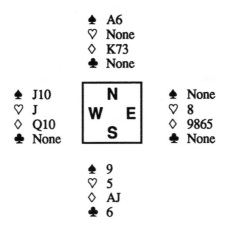

```
              ♠ A6
              ♡ None
              ◊ K73
              ♣ None
  ♠ J10      ┌─────────┐    ♠ None
  ♡ J        │    N    │    ♡ 8
  ◊ Q10      │ W     E │    ◊ 9865
  ♣ None     │    S    │    ♣ None
             └─────────┘
              ♠ 9
              ♡ 5
              ◊ AJ
              ♣ 6
```

This is the same situation as in diagram (92). On the lead of the six of clubs, West cannot discard a spade, otherwise dummy will make two spade tricks. Neither can he discard a diamond, or South will make two diamonds and dummy one diamond and a spade. Therefore West has to discard the jack of hearts. Dummy discards the six of spades and now the lead of a spade squeezes East in hearts and diamonds.

If, in diagram (91), the positions of the clash menace and one-card double menace are reversed, we arrive at another situation:

(93)

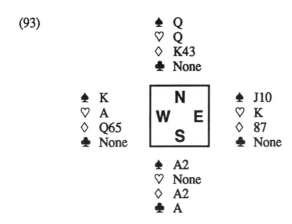

```
              ♠ Q
              ♡ Q
              ◊ K43
              ♣ None
  ♠ K        ┌─────────┐    ♠ J10
  ♡ A        │    N    │    ♡ K
  ◊ Q65      │ W     E │    ◊ 87
  ♣ None     │    S    │    ♣ None
             └─────────┘
              ♠ A2
              ♡ None
              ◊ A2
              ♣ A
```

151

Here the spade suit is a clash menace against West with the longer part in front of him. On the lead of the ace of clubs, West is clash-squeezed and has to discard the ace of hearts. North throws a diamond. The ace of diamonds is played, and, at the next trick, the king of diamonds squeezes East in spades and hearts.

The next hand is an example.

North-South game; Dealer West

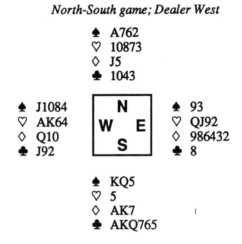

```
           ♠  A762
           ♡  10873
           ◊  J5
           ♣  1043

 ♠  J1084      N        ♠  93
 ♡  AK64    W     E     ♡  QJ92
 ◊  Q10                 ◊  986432
 ♣  J92        S        ♣  8

           ♠  KQ5
           ♡  5
           ◊  AK7
           ♣  AKQ765
```

South becomes declarer at a contract of six clubs after an opening bid of one spade by West. The opening lead is the king of hearts on which East plays the queen. A small heart to the seven and nine is ruffed by South.

If the trumps break 2-2, there is no problem, but two rounds of clubs reveal the position. The king of diamonds is played, dropping West's ten. The declarer has reason to believe that West held originally at most two cards in diamonds, his hand pattern may be 5-3-2-3 or 4-4-2-3 (or even 5-4-1-3, in this case the contract cannot be made). Therefore, a ruff of the third diamond in dummy is out of the question.

Bearing in mind the non-simultaneous double clash squeeze in diagram (93), the declarer reasons that if West has just one diamond left and this card is the queen—very likely in view of West's opening bid—the squeeze can be executed.

The declarer now plays two more rounds of trumps and this is the position:

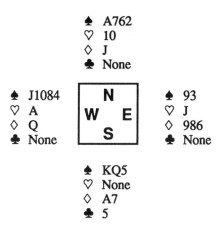

The last trump is played squeezing West, who has to discard the ace of hearts. North throws a spade. The king, queen and ace of spades are played and on the ace of spades East is squeezed in hearts and diamonds.

An interesting feature of the above hand is that even if West holds originally three diamonds to the queen (with four spades, three hearts and three clubs) the hand can still be made with out the risk of ruffing the third diamond in dummy. If West discards a diamond on the fourth-round trump lead, the situation is exactly the same as before. If West chooses to unguard the heart suit, the situation at trick eight will be this:

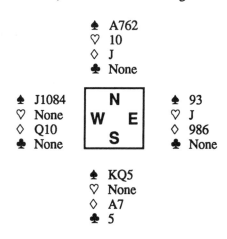

As before, the declarer plays the last trump. The order of declarer's play is not changed, but this time the situation becomes that of a non-simultaneous double positional squeeze, and in this case nothing will be lost if the king and queen of spades are both cashed before the last trump is played. However, before South's last top spade is cashed, the declarer must make sure that by that time only East can guard the heart suit.

In each of diagrams (91), (92) and (93) there is a one-card double menace. Such a menace is very rarely encountered in squeezes of other types. In fact, we have seen it displaying its function only in diagrams (43) and (47) when we were looking at double triple squeezes and in some of the guard-squeeze situations. Viewed in this way, we see a similarity between the guard squeeze and the clash squeeze.

It is easy to see that the squeeze in diagram (93) fails if the ace of diamonds is played before the ace of clubs (West simply discards the king of spades on the ace of clubs). But in this case an extension of the one-card double menace to a split two-card double menace will provide an entry to the South hand and hence give rise to a new situation:

(94)

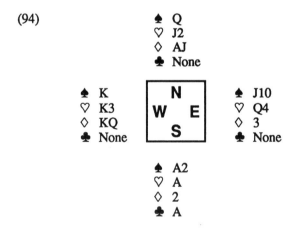

```
                  ♠  Q
                  ♡  J2
                  ◇  AJ
                  ♣  None

    ♠  K          ┌─────────┐      ♠  J10
    ♡  K3         │    N    │      ♡  Q4
    ◇  KQ         │ W     E │      ◇  3
    ♣  None       │    S    │      ♣  None
                  └─────────┘
                  ♠  A2
                  ♡  A
                  ◇  2
                  ♣  A
```

West is clash-squeezed on the lead of the ace of clubs and must unguard the heart suit. North lets go of the jack of diamonds. The ace of hearts is now cashed and, at the next trick, East is simple-squeezed when the two of diamonds is led to the ace.

The next hand is played by South in three no-trumps. By recognising the position, eleven tricks can be made without much difficulty.

154

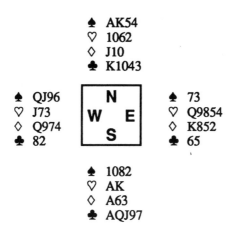

```
          ♠ AK54
          ♡ 1062
          ◇ J10
          ♣ K1043
♠ QJ96      N      ♠ 73
♡ J73    W     E   ♡ Q9854
◇ Q974      S      ◇ K852
♣ 82               ♣ 65
          ♠ 1082
          ♡ AK
          ◇ A63
          ♣ AQJ97
```

West leads the queen of spades, which is ducked by South. The four of diamonds is led, at trick two, East's king winning. East returns the spade (lucky for South the return is not a diamond) to the eight, nine and king. The declarer then plays the ace of hearts and four rounds of clubs. On the fourth round of clubs, if West unguards the heart suit, the king of hearts may be cashed to leave this non-simultaneous double-squeeze situation:

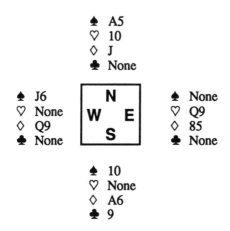

```
          ♠ A5
          ♡ 10
          ◇ J
          ♣ None
♠ J6        N      ♠ None
♡ None   W     E   ♡ Q9
◇ Q9        S      ◇ 85
♣ None             ♣ None
          ♠ 10
          ♡ None
          ◇ A6
          ♣ 9
```

If instead West bares his queen of diamonds on the fourth-round club lead, the position is similar to that of diagram (94):

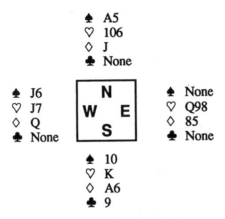

The lead of the nine of clubs begins the clash squeeze against West. In this situation South should not make the mistake of playing the king of hearts before the nine of clubs, for that would allow West to discard the diamond on the nine of clubs.

The position in diagram (94) has a parallel shown in the next diagram:

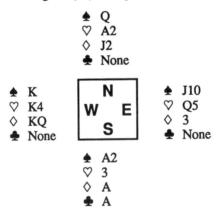

But this is only a variation of a commonly-encountered position of an ordinary double squeeze. Both the ace of spades and the ace of diamonds can be played first. The position then reduces to that of diagram (15).

We will present one more basic form of the non-simultaneous double clash squeeze with the clash squeeze against the opponent to the left of the squeeze-card. If in the last diagram the clash menace is of three-card length and split, then the ace of hearts may be played earlier:

(95)

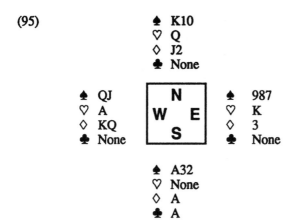

♠ K10
♡ Q
◇ J2
♣ None

♠ QJ　　　　N　　　♠ 987
♡ A　　　W　　E　♡ K
◇ KQ　　　　　　　◇ 3
♣ None　　　S　　　♣ None

♠ A32
♡ None
◇ A
♣ A

The lead of the ace of clubs clash-squeezes West. He is forced to throw the ace of hearts. North lets go of a diamond and, at the next trick, the ace of diamonds squeezes East in spades and hearts.

Let us study this hand dealt by South at love all.

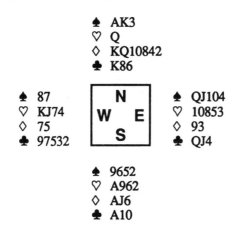

♠ AK3
♡ Q
◇ KQ10842
♣ K86

♠ 87　　　　N　　　♠ QJ104
♡ KJ74　　W　　E　♡ 10853
◇ 75　　　　　　　◇ 93
♣ 97532　　S　　　♣ QJ4

♠ 9652
♡ A962
◇ AJ6
♣ A10

South	North
1NT	3◇
3♡	4NT
5♠	6NT
Pass	

South, using the non-vulnerable weak no-trump, first rebids his heart suit and then shows three aces in reply to North's Blackwood four no-trumps. West leads the eight of spades on which North plays low, East's ten winning. The return is the three of hearts, which South wins with the ace.

Four rounds of diamonds are played, the East-West discards are quite easy. A fifth diamond is led. East must guard the spade suit. If East discards his last heart, the declarer plays off the ace and king of spades and makes the contract by an ordinary double squeeze. The end position is this:

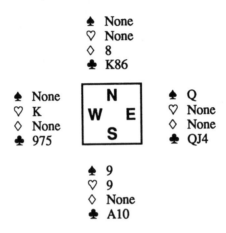

If East discards the four of clubs on the fifth diamond, the declarer plays a spade, leaving this position:

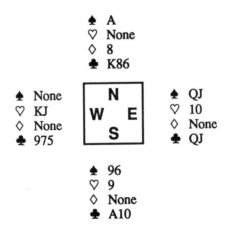

This is the same double-clash-squeeze situation as in diagram (95). The eight of diamonds is led, and East is clash-squeezed. If he throws a club, the ace, ten and king of clubs will be made in turn, using the ace of spades as the entry. East must therefore part with the ten of hearts. South discards a spade and West a heart. The ace of spades is then played, squeezing West in hearts and clubs.

The situations in diagrams (91)-(95) are basic forms of non-simultaneous double clash squeeze. In each of these situations, North-South have four winners out of five cards. The squeeze-cards are all in the South hand, and the clash menaces all against West. The clash squeeze against West comes first, and the simple squeeze against East takes place at a later trick. Furthermore, the situations are all positional; the squeeze fails when the East-West cards are reversed.

We now state the requirements as follows:

Diagram (91)—A clash menace and a split three-card menace against West with the longer parts in the North hand; a one-card double menace in the South hand.

Diagram (92)—A split three-card clash menace and a two-card menace against West with the longer parts in the North hand; a one-card double menace in the South hand.

Diagram (93)—A clash menace with the longer part in the South hand; a one-card double menace in the North hand; a split three-card menace against West with the three-card part in the North hand.

Diagram (94)—A clash menace with the longer part in the South hand; a split two-card double menace with the master card in the South hand; a two-card menace against West in the North hand.

Diagram (95)—A split three-card clash menace with the longer part in the South hand; a one-card double menace in the North hand; a split two-card menace against West with the master card in the South hand.

In these double clash squeezes, the clash squeezes are all against West. Mr Yang Guozhu, of the People's University of China, has discovered a non-simultaneous double clash squeeze with the clash squeeze against East.

Love all; Dealer South[*]

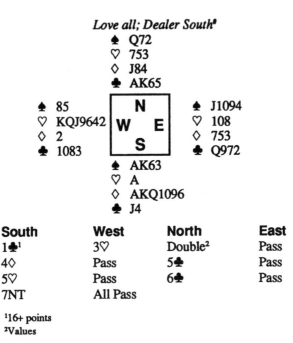

	♠ Q72	
	♡ 753	
	◇ J84	
	♣ AK65	

South	West	North	East
1♣[1]	3♡	Double[2]	Pass
4◇	Pass	5♣	Pass
5♡	Pass	6♣	Pass
7NT	All Pass		

[1]16+ points
[2]Values

West leads the king of hearts, South's ace winning. The declarer cashes the king of clubs and plays five rounds of diamonds, North discarding a heart and a club.

If East discards the heart on the fifth round of diamonds, the declarer makes the contract through an ordinary double squeeze. If East discards a club, the situation becomes:

(96)

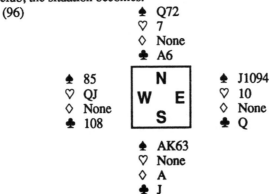

[*] *Bridge Quarterly* (Chinese), 1990, No.3; also, *The Bridge World,* June 1990.

This is a non-simultaneous double clash squeeze. On the lead of the ace of diamonds, North throws a spade, and East is clash-squeezed and has to let go of the ten of hearts to prevent South from gaining an immediate extra trick. The queen, king and ace of spades are played in turn, and West is squeezed in hearts and clubs on the lead of the ace of spades.

If the opening lead against the seven no-trump contract is a spade, South's king wins. South cashes dummy's king of clubs and plays five rounds of diamonds. In order to retain a stopper in hearts, East has to bare his queen of clubs. This is the position:

(97)

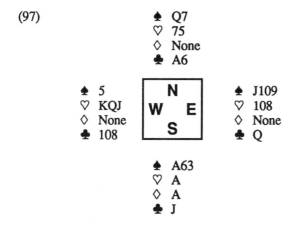

```
                ♠ Q7
                ♡ 75
                ◇ None
                ♣ A6

    ♠ 5          N          ♠ J109
    ♡ KQJ     W     E       ♡ 108
    ◇ None       S          ◇ None
    ♣ 108                    ♣ Q

                ♠ A63
                ♡ A
                ◇ A
                ♣ J
```

This is another non-simultaneous double clash squeeze with the clash squeeze against East. The North-South club combination is a two-card clash menace against East, the spade suit is a split three-card menace against East, and the heart suit is a split two-card double menace.

On the lead of the ace of diamonds, North discards the seven of spades, and East is clash-squeezed. A spade discard enables South to make three spade tricks with the ace of hearts as the entry. The discard of the queen of clubs permits South to win the jack and ace of clubs separately, using the queen of spades as an entry. And if East discards a heart, South plays the queen of spades, the ace of hearts and the ace of spades in turn, squeezing West in hearts and clubs at trick 11.

The following situation was discovered by Wang Zhonghua:[*]

(98)

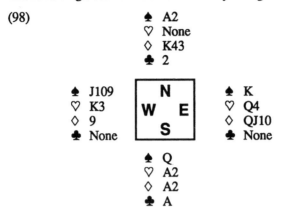

The spade suit in the North-South hands is a clash menace against East, the diamond suit is a split three-card menace against East, and the heart suit is a two-card double menace.

On the lead of the ace of clubs, East is clash-squeezed and discards a heart. West will be squeezed in spades and hearts at a later trick.

This situation is a non-simultaneous automatic double clash squeeze. If the East and West hands are interchanged, West will be clash-squeezed and East simple-squeezed.

This is another form of the non-simultaneous automatic double clash squeeze:

(99)

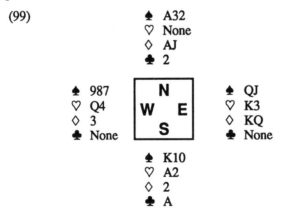

* *Bridge Quarterly* (Chinese), 1991, No. 1.

On the lead of the ace of clubs, West discards the three of diamonds, and East is clash-squeezed. East discards a heart (best), but West is simple-squeezed in spades and hearts on the lead of the ace of diamonds.

8.3 Simultaneous double clash squeezes

We now propose to discuss the simultaneous double clash squeeze.

The first situation is one that combines a clash menace against West with an ordinary split three-card double menace:

(100)

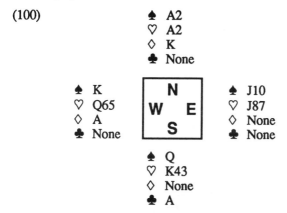

	♠ A2
	♡ A2
	◊ K
	♣ None

♠ K		♠ J10
♡ Q65		♡ J87
◊ A		◊ None
♣ None		♣ None

	♠ Q
	♡ K43
	◊ None
	♣ A

But this situation can usually be reduced to an ordinary double squeeze by an earlier play of the ace of spades. The result is the situation in diagram (16).

If, in this diagram, the clash menace is replaced by a split three-card clash menace, we see that the king of hearts can be played first. This gives rise to a basic form of the simultaneous double clash squeeze.

(101)

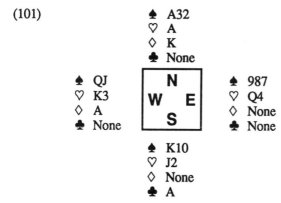

	♠ A32
	♡ A
	◊ K
	♣ None

♠ QJ		♠ 987
♡ K3		♡ Q4
◊ A		◊ None
♣ None		♣ None

	♠ K10
	♡ J2
	◊ None
	♣ A

163

On the lead of the ace of clubs, West is clash-squeezed and is forced to unguard the heart suit. North discards the king of diamonds, and East is caught in a automatic simple squeeze.

This is illustrated in the following hand.

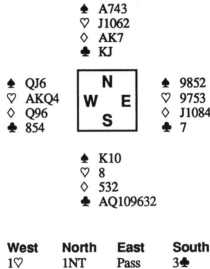

```
                    ♠ A743
                    ♡ J1062
                    ◇ AK7
                    ♣ KJ

    ♠ QJ6          ┌─────────┐          ♠ 9852
    ♡ AKQ4         │    N    │          ♡ 9753
    ◇ Q96          │  W   E  │          ◇ J1084
    ♣ 854          │    S    │          ♣ 7
                   └─────────┘
                    ♠ K10
                    ♡ 8
                    ◇ 532
                    ♣ AQ109632
```

West	North	East	South
1♡	1NT	Pass	3♣
Pass	3♠	Pass	4♣
Pass	4◇	Pass	5♣
Pass	6♣	All Pass	

West leads the king and then the ace of hearts, which South ruffs. Three rounds of clubs are played, dummy discarding a spade. A diamond is led to the king and a heart led and ruffed. The declarer plays another club, on which dummy discards the seven of diamonds. At this trick, West faces the choice of unguarding the diamonds or baring the spade honours. If he unguards the diamond suit, the declarer plays the ace of diamonds and king of spades and makes the contract through an ordinary double squeeze. The end position is this:

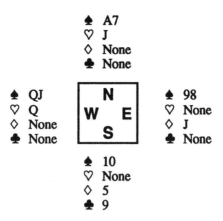

```
        ♠  A7
        ♡  J
        ◊  None
        ♣  None

♠ QJ      ┌─────────┐      ♠ 98
♡ Q       │   N     │      ♡ None
◊ None    │ W     E │      ◊ J
♣ None    │   S     │      ♣ None
          └─────────┘
        ♠  10
        ♡  None
        ◊  5
        ♣  9
```

The opponents are squeezed simultaneously on the lead of the nine of clubs. When West throws a spade, North has no further use for the jack of hearts. East is now squeezed in spades and diamonds.

If West adopts the course of baring his spade honours instead of unguarding the diamond suit at trick eight, the declarer makes the contract through a double clash squeeze. The end position at the next trick is:

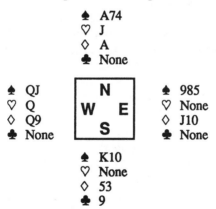

```
        ♠  A74
        ♡  J
        ◊  A
        ♣  None

♠ QJ      ┌─────────┐      ♠ 985
♡ Q       │   N     │      ♡ None
◊ Q9      │ W     E │      ◊ J10
♣ None    │   S     │      ♣ None
          └─────────┘
        ♠  K10
        ♡  None
        ◊  53
        ♣  9
```

On the lead of the nine of clubs, West is clash-squeezed, and East simple-squeezed. West's only safe discard is a diamond, whereupon North's jack of hearts is discarded, and East is squeezed in spades and diamonds.

The contract can also be made through a double ruffing clash squeeze (the double ruffing clash squeeze will be discussed later).

A similar situation can be set up by reversing the positions of the clash menace and the double menace in diagram (101) .

(102)

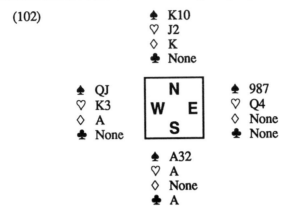

```
              ♠  K10
              ♡  J2
              ◇  K
              ♣  None

♠ QJ         ┌─────────┐        ♠ 987
♡ K3         │    N    │        ♡ Q4
◇ A          │ W     E │        ◇ None
♣ None       │    S    │        ♣ None
             └─────────┘
              ♠  A32
              ♡  A
              ◇  None
              ♣  A
```

On the lead of the ace of clubs, West is subjected to a clash squeeze and East a simple squeeze. It is clear that West's only discard to keep the game alive is a heart, whereupon North's king of diamonds is discarded, and East is squeezed in spades and hearts.

It is easy to see that in both (101) and (102) the squeeze fails if either the king of spades or the ace of hearts is played before leading the ace of clubs. If the king of spades is played at an earlier stage, both West and East can safely discard in hearts on the lead of the ace of clubs. And if the ace of hearts has been played at an earlier stage, then, to avoid conceding an extra trick, West must discard in spades and East in hearts when the ace of clubs is led.

In the next hand South is the dealer.

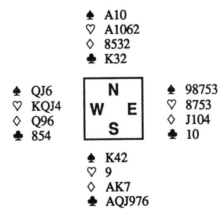

```
              ♠  A10
              ♡  A1062
              ◇  8532
              ♣  K32

♠ QJ6        ┌─────────┐        ♠ 98753
♡ KQJ4       │    N    │        ♡ 8753
◇ Q96        │ W     E │        ◇ J104
♣ 854        │    S    │        ♣ 10
             └─────────┘
              ♠  K42
              ♡  9
              ◇  AK7
              ♣  AQJ976
```

South	North
1♣	1♡
3♣	4♣
4NT [1]	5♡
6NT	Pass

[1]Blackwood

West leads the king of hearts. The declarer ducks, to come to an "all-but-one" position. West continues with the queen of hearts, which dummy's ace wins, South discarding the seven of diamonds. The clubs are then played off.

On the lead of the fifth club, if West unguards the diamond suit, the declarer cashes the ace and king of diamonds, leaving the following four-card ending:

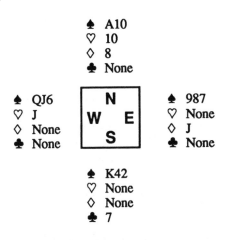

```
              ♠  A10
              ♡  10
              ◇  8
              ♣  None

  ♠  QJ6      ┌───────┐      ♠  987
  ♡  J        │   N   │      ♡  None
  ◇  None     │ W   E │      ◇  J
  ♣  None     │   S   │      ♣  None
              └───────┘
              ♠  K42
              ♡  None
              ◇  None
              ♣  7
```

This is an ordinary simultaneous-double-squeeze situation, the seven of clubs being the squeeze-card.

In case West retains the diamond stopper and bares his spade honours on the fifth club, the declarer cashes a diamond winner and produces this position:

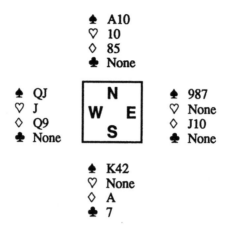

♠ A10
♥ 10
♦ 85
♣ None

♠ QJ   ♠ 987
♥ J   ♥ None
♦ Q9   ♦ J10
♣ None   ♣ None

♠ K42
♥ None
♦ A
♣ 7

This is the same simultaneous-double-clash-squeeze situation as in diagram (102). On the lead of the seven of clubs, West is clash-squeezed and East simple-squeezed.

It must be noted that the situations in diagrams (101) and (102) are both positional: if the East-West cards are interchanged, West will throw a heart on the lead of the ace of clubs, but North will have no suitable discard at this stage.

It is also to be pointed out that in these diagrams the one-card menace against West may be increased to two cards without altering the effectiveness of the squeeze. But, in this event, the situation becomes non-simultaneous, as East will have an idle card to throw on the lead of the ace of clubs. Moreover, if in diagram (101) the one-card menace against West is increased to two cards, then the ace of hearts may be played earlier, reducing the situation to that of diagram (92). Similarly, if in diagram (102) the one-card menace against West is replaced by a split two-card menace with the master card in the South hand, then the ace of hearts can be played first and the situation becomes that of diagram (95).

168

8.4 Double clash squeezes of other types

We shall make a further discussion of the situation in diagram (89), repeated below:

(89)

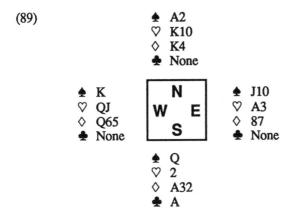

In this diagram, if both the king and ace of diamonds are played before leading the ace of clubs, the position becomes:

(103)

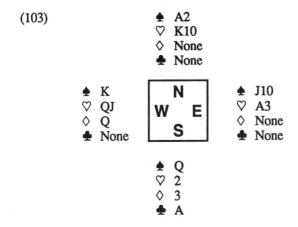

It seems at first sight as if there is no squeeze since no entry is left to the North hand except in the suit of the clash menace. In fact, this is a basic end position of the simultaneous double clash squeeze.

On the lead of the ace of clubs, West cannot discard the queen of diamonds. If West throws the king of spades, North discards the ten of hearts and East is squeezed. He must retain the length in spades, so has to bare the ace of hearts. The queen of spades is taken and a heart lead throws East in to concede the last trick to North's ace of spades.

If West discards a heart on the ace of clubs, North lets go of the two of spades. The two of hearts is now led to the king and ace, establishing North's ten. There is no diamond for East to lead and he must concede the last two tricks to North's ten of hearts and ace of spades.

This is an unusual double-clash-squeeze situation. We recall that all the clash squeezes considered so far have been based on the requirement that an additional entry is kept to the hand with the longer part of the clash menace.

Diagram (103) is not so. There is no extra entry to the hand with the longer part of the clash menace, and yet the combination of the cards enables North-South to set up a trick after the squeeze, provided that the correct discard is made in the North hand when the ace of clubs is led.

In this diagram, as in all other basic clash-squeeze situations, it is noticed that the squeeze fails if South holds a small spade instead of the queen. When this is the case, West can throw the king of spades on the ace of clubs, and East discards in the same suit as North.

Note that East-West have two immediate winners, and, if West has the lead, they can even win three tricks. But South's lead of the ace of clubs restricts them to only one trick.

The ending in diagram (103) is illustrated in the next hand.

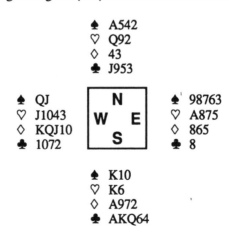

The contract is three no-trumps by South. West leads three rounds of diamonds, South's ace wins the third, dummy discarding a spade. How can the contract be made with an overtrick?

The declarer takes the ace-king-jack of clubs and leads the two of hearts from dummy. East has to duck and South's king wins. The declarer now plays the queen of clubs and the king of spades, leaving this position:

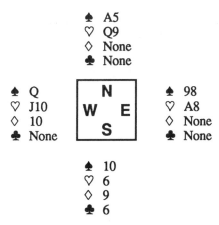

```
                  ♠ A5
                  ♡ Q9
                  ◇ None
                  ♣ None
     ♠ Q        ┌─────────┐     ♠ 98
     ♡ J10      │    N    │     ♡ A8
     ◇ 10       │  W   E  │     ◇ None
     ♣ None     │    S    │     ♣ None
               └─────────┘
                  ♠ 10
                  ♡ 6
                  ◇ 9
                  ♣ 6
```

The last club is led and the opponents are squeezed simultaneously. The situation is the same as in diagram (103).

We see that in diagram (103) the longer part of the clash menace is not allowed to be transferred to the South hand:

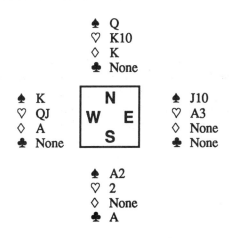

```
                  ♠ Q
                  ♡ K10
                  ◇ K
                  ♣ None
     ♠ K        ┌─────────┐     ♠ J10
     ♡ QJ       │    N    │     ♡ A3
     ◇ A        │  W   E  │     ◇ None
     ♣ None     │    S    │     ♣ None
               └─────────┘
                  ♠ A2
                  ♡ 2
                  ◇ None
                  ♣ A
```

On the lead of the ace of clubs, West discards either in hearts or in diamonds. North lets go of the king of diamonds, and East the three of hearts. Although a heart winner can then be established, there is no entry to the North hand to cash it. North-South are restricted to two tricks out of the remaining four cards, provided that West retains the king of spades on the lead of the ace of clubs. (If West throws the king of spades on the ace of clubs, North discards the king of diamonds and East is forced to bare his ace of hearts. Now either the king of hearts can be set up with the queen of spades as the entry to cash it or the queen and ace of spades can be made separately.)

However, if the one-card menace against West in the last diagram is replaced by a two-card menace, the position is quite different and a new double-clash-squeeze position arises:

(104)

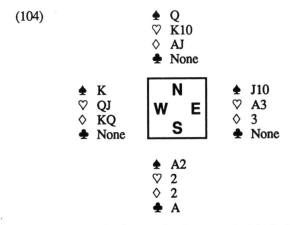

```
                    ♠ Q
                    ♡ K10
                    ◊ AJ
                    ♣ None
    ♠ K         ┌─────────┐      ♠ J10
    ♡ QJ        │    N    │      ♡ A3
    ◊ KQ        │  W   E  │      ◊ 3
    ♣ None      │    S    │      ♣ None
                └─────────┘
                    ♠ A2
                    ♡ 2
                    ◊ 2
                    ♣ A
```

This is an example of a non-simultaneous double clash squeeze. On the lead of the ace of clubs, West is clash-squeezed. A diamond discard immediately sets up the jack; a heart discard permits South to throw North's jack of diamonds and lead the two of hearts to the king and ace, establishing the ten. So West has to discard his king of spades. North lets go of the jack of diamonds (or the ten of hearts) and East the three of diamonds. The ace of diamonds is played, East is simple-squeezed and has to throw the three of hearts. The queen of spades is then cashed and a heart led. East is put on lead and must give the last trick to South's ace of spades.

South should not make the mistake of cashing the queen of spades before the ace of diamonds, otherwise East would escape from the throw-in play by getting rid of his last spade on the ace of diamonds. Actually, the ace of diamonds is a squeeze-card to East, forcing him to bare the ace of hearts.

In the following hand, the declarer can win eleven tricks by recognising the position.

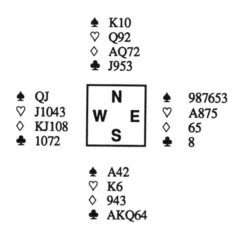

Against South's three no-trumps, West leads the jack of diamonds, which is allowed to hold. At trick two, the queen of spades is led and won in dummy. The two of hearts is led to South's king, the diamond finesse is taken and the clubs are played. At trick nine, the position is:

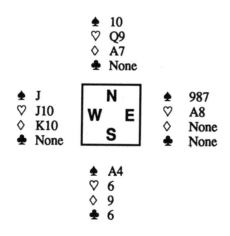

The lead of the six of clubs squeezes West, who must discard the jack of spades. North throws the seven of diamonds and East the seven of spades. The ace of diamonds is played, forcing East to bare the ace of hearts. After the ten of spades is cashed, East is thrown in with the ace of hearts and South's ace of spades wins the last trick.

8.5 *Single ruffing clash squeezes*

In all the clash-squeeze situations dealt with up to now, the ruffing power of the trump suit has played no part.

In a clash squeeze, if one of the menaces is a ruffing menace, the squeeze will be called a ruffing clash squeeze. The ruffing clash squeeze will be classified as single or double according to whether one or both opponents are involved in the squeeze.

The following, with clubs as trumps, is the simplest form of single ruffing clash squeeze:

(105)

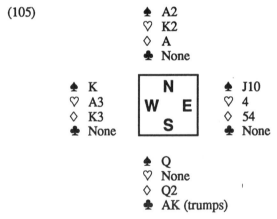

	♠ A2	
	♡ K2	
	◇ A	
	♣ None	

♠ K		♠ J10
♡ A3		♡ 4
◇ K3		◇ 54
♣ None		♣ None

	♠ Q	
	♡ None	
	◇ Q2	
	♣ AK (trumps)	

South leads the ace of clubs and West is squeezed. The discard of the king of spades will enable North-South to make the queen and ace separately, using the ace of diamonds as an entry. The discard of the three of hearts will permit South to throw the two of spades and enter dummy with an ace, ruffing out the king of hearts, with the other ace as the entry to make it. While if the three of diamonds is discarded, North's ace drops the king and South still has a ruffing entry to cash the queen of diamonds. Hence, in whatever suit West might discard, an additional trick is bound to be set up for North-South.

In this situation, West is threatened in three suits. The spade suit in the North-South hands is a clash menace, the heart suit a ruffing menace, and the diamond suit a split two-card single menace, all against West.

It seems that this diagram describes quite well the nature of a single ruffing clash squeeze and that the squeeze is effective solely because West is forced to discard before North. We might well be led to the conclusion that this is a positional single ruffing clash squeeze and the squeeze fails when the West and East hands are interchanged.

However, if we recognise the fundamental principle of the ruffing squeeze, a further consideration will show that the situation in diagram (105) is not basic.

On the lead of the ace of clubs, if West discards the king of spades, North might choose to throw the two of spades to arrive at this position:

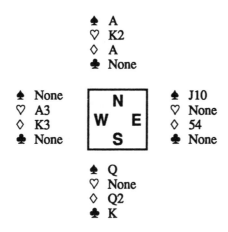

```
              ♠ A
              ♡ K2
              ◇ A
              ♣ None

  ♠ None    ┌─────────┐    ♠ J10
  ♡ A3      │    N    │    ♡ None
  ◇ K3      │ W     E │    ◇ 54
  ♣ None    │    S    │    ♣ None
            └─────────┘
              ♠ Q
              ♡ None
              ◇ Q2
              ♣ K
```

Now the queen of spades is led to the ace and West is again squeezed, this time in a single-ruffing situation. Moreover, the squeeze is equally effective if the West and East hands are interchanged. The situation is the same as in diagram (59).

The situation in diagram (105) is, therefore, only a variation of the above automatic situation, which is the commonest of the single ruffing squeeze.

By introducing a three-card ruffing menace, an entry to the North hand is thus provided in the ruffing-menace suit itself, and we arrive at a true single-ruffing-clash-squeeze situation shown in the next diagram:

(106)

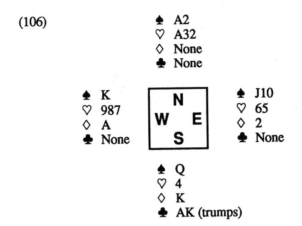

```
              ♠  A2
              ♡  A32
              ◊  None
              ♣  None
   ♠  K      ┌──────┐     ♠  J10
   ♡  987    │  N   │     ♡  65
   ◊  A      │W    E│     ◊  2
   ♣  None   │  S   │     ♣  None
            └──────┘
              ♠  Q
              ♡  4
              ◊  K
              ♣  AK (trumps)
```

There are three menaces, all against West. The spade suit is a clash menace, the heart suit is a three-card ruffing menace with an entry to the North hand, and the king of diamonds is a one-card single menace.

When the ace of clubs is led, West is squeezed in a ruffing-clash situation. If he discards the ace of diamonds, South's king of diamonds becomes a winner. If he discards the king of spades, the queen and ace will be made separately, the ace of hearts being an entry to the North hand. And if he discards a heart, North throws the two of spades. The ace of hearts is played and the two of hearts led and ruffed, establishing the three. Now all North's cards are good.

It must be noted that in this diagram the clash menace is essential. The squeeze fails when South holds a small spade instead of the queen.

The situation is positional. If the West and East hands are interchanged, East simply discards in whichever suit North lets go and no squeeze is available.

The following hand illustrates the end position in (106):

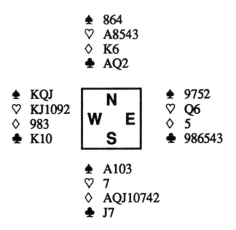

```
                    ♠ 864
                    ♡ A8543
                    ◇ K6
                    ♣ AQ2

   ♠ KQJ                        ♠ 9752
   ♡ KJ1092       N             ♡ Q6
   ◇ 983       W     E          ◇ 5
   ♣ K10          S             ♣ 986543

                    ♠ A103
                    ♡ 7
                    ◇ AQJ10742
                    ♣ J7
```

The bidding:

West	North	East	South
1♡	Pass	Pass	3◇
Pass	3♡	Pass	4◇
Pass	4NT	Pass	5♡
Pass	6◇	All Pass	

The opening lead is the king of spades. Assuming a successful finesse in clubs, the declarer counts only eleven tricks. Hence the first trick is ducked, in preparation for a possible squeeze. West continues with the queen of spades, South winning with the ace.

The declarer's first and natural thought is to draw trumps, ruff one or two rounds of hearts and hope for West to hold the long clubs, including the king, so that a simple or triple squeeze might operate against him. But in view of the fact that West has made an opening bid of one heart and that he has played the king, queen of spades already, it would hardly be possible that he should hold in addition six or more clubs. Some other way has to be found to make the contract, if it can be made at all.

The jack of spades seems likely to be with West. And since West has not switched to a heart at trick two, the assumption may be made that he does not hold both the king and queen in that suit. What happens if West holds five or more hearts, in addition to the jack of spades and king of clubs? The declarer reasons that, in this case, West can be squeezed in a single-ruffing-clash situation in the end game.

Five rounds of trumps are played leaving this position:

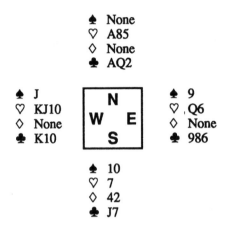

The declarer now plays the four of diamonds on which West is squeezed. Any discard will enable South to set up an extra trick and make the contract. The situation is similar to that of diagram (106), only that the length of the clash menace (the club suit) is increased by one card.

If, for example, West discards a heart, South discards dummy's two of clubs. A heart is led to the ace, a heart is ruffed and the club finesse is taken. Dummy's remaining heart is a winner and enables South to discard his losing spade.

A review of the hand shows that if West switches to a heart at trick two, it would be much easier for South to fulfill the contract. The declarer simply ruffs a heart, draws the outstanding trumps, takes the finesse in clubs, ruffs another heart to make sure that East has no more hearts, and then plays off all the remaining trumps. Dummy retains the ace of clubs as well as a spade and a heart. At trick 11, the club is led to the North hand, and West is simple-squeezed in spades and hearts.

In diagram (106), if the one-card menace is increased in length, the squeeze is, of course, still effective. And, in this event, the situation becomes automatic, that is, the East-West hands can be reversed:

(107)

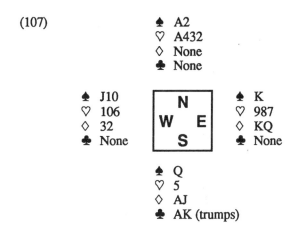

♠ A2
♥ A432
♦ None
♣ None

♠ J10
♥ 106
♦ 32
♣ None

♠ K
♥ 987
♦ KQ
♣ None

♠ Q
♥ 5
♦ AJ
♣ AK (trumps)

The ace of clubs is led, and East is squeezed in a ruffing-clash situation.

Although diagram (107) has its value, we do not consider it a basic situation. For, if the ace of spades is cashed earlier, then the play of both the ace of diamonds and the ace of clubs, on which North discards two small hearts, reduces the situation to an ordinary positional double squeeze.

But the situation in either (106) or (107) cannot be reduced to a simple squeeze. In other words, a simple squeeze against the clash-menaced opponent in hearts and diamonds (by an earlier play of the ace of spades as a stripping process) does not work, as his partner also holds protection in the heart suit. The heart suit in (106) and (107) is, therefore, not to be treated as a single menace. It may be described as a semi-double menace.

8.6 Double ruffing clash squeezes

We have seen that diagram (105) is a variation of an ordinary single ruffing squeeze. When East also holds protection in the suit of the ordinary menace, that is, in diamonds, a basic end position of the double ruffing clash squeeze is set up:

(108)

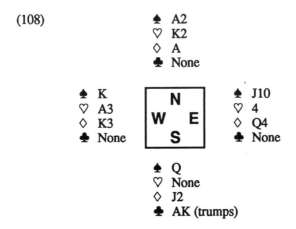

```
              ♠  A2
              ♡  K2
              ◊  A
              ♣  None

♠  K                        ♠  J10
♡  A3          N            ♡  4
◊  K3       W     E         ◊  Q4
♣  None        S            ♣  None

              ♠  Q
              ♡  None
              ◊  J2
              ♣  AK (trumps)
```

Here the spade suit is a clash menace and the heart suit a ruffing menace, both against West; the diamond suit is a split two-card double menace. On the lead of the ace of clubs, West is ruffing-clash squeezed and has to discard a diamond. North and East both throw a heart. A diamond is led to the ace, and North plays the last heart, which South ruffs. At this trick, East is squeezed in spades and diamonds.

The next hand is an example.

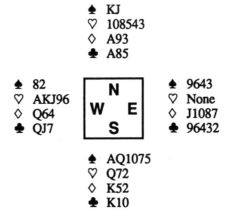

```
              ♠  KJ
              ♡  108543
              ◊  A93
              ♣  A85

♠  82                       ♠  9643
♡  AKJ96       N            ♡  None
◊  Q64      W     E         ◊  J1087
♣  QJ7         S            ♣  96432

              ♠  AQ1075
              ♡  Q72
              ◊  K52
              ♣  K10
```

The contract is four spades by South. West leads the king and then the ace of hearts on which East lets go of two clubs. A third round of hearts is led and ruffed by East. The return is the jack of diamonds, won with the king. A spade is led to the king, the jack is returned and overtaken with the ace. At trick seven, the queen of spades is played, drawing East's last trump and at the same time beginning the squeeze against West. With two vital entries in dummy, West cannot afford to throw a heart. If he throws a diamond, the declarer makes the contract through an ordinary double squeeze. The end position is this:

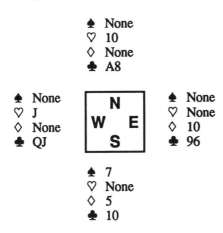

The lead of the seven of spades squeezes West and East simultaneously.

If, at trick seven, West discards the seven of clubs on the queen of spades, North must throw the small diamond. The king of clubs is then played, dropping West's jack. The position is:

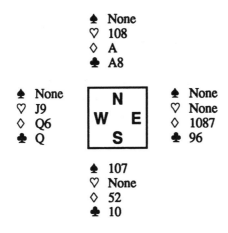

The declarer plays the ten of spades, which squeezes West in a ruffing-clash situation. West has to unguard the diamond suit. North throws a heart and East a diamond. The ace of diamonds is cashed and dummy's last heart is led and ruffed, squeezing East in diamonds and clubs. Hence the contract is made, in this case, by means of a double ruffing clash squeeze.

The following hand was discussed earlier in this chapter:

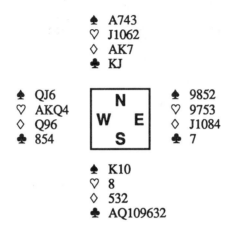

```
              ♠ A743
              ♡ J1062
              ◊ AK7
              ♣ KJ

  ♠ QJ6           N        ♠ 9852
  ♡ AKQ4      W      E     ♡ 9753
  ◊ Q96           S        ◊ J1084
  ♣ 854                    ♣ 7

              ♠ K10
              ♡ 8
              ◊ 532
              ♣ AQ109632
```

Against South's six clubs, West leads the king and then the ace of hearts, which South ruffs.

It was pointed out that the declarer makes the contract through an ordinary double squeeze or a double clash squeeze according to West's defence. I also said that the contract can be made through a double ruffing clash squeeze if West bares his spade honours on the fourth round of trumps.

Having had a clear view of the ruffing clash squeeze in our mind, it is now easily seen that, after ruffing the heart, the declarer will arrive at exactly the same ending as in diagram (108) by playing four rounds of trumps (West discarding a spade and North a spade and a diamond), followed by the king of diamonds and king of spades. At this point, another club lead begins the double ruffing clash squeeze against West. The position, at trick nine, is:

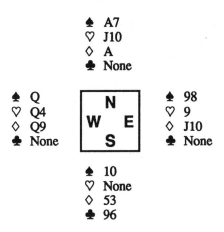

The nine of clubs is led. If West discards the queen of spades, South's ten and North's ace of spades make two tricks. If West discards the four of hearts, a heart trick can be ruffed out in the North hand. If West discards a diamond, North and East both throw a heart. A diamond is led to the ace and the last heart led and ruffed, squeezing East in spades and diamonds.

In diagram (106), if East also guards the diamond suit, a second form of the double ruffing clash squeeze arises:

(109)

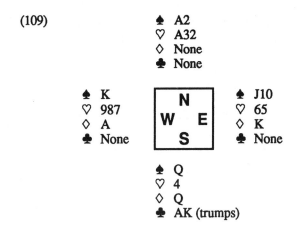

In this diagram, the queen of diamonds is a one-card double menace against both opponents.

The ace of clubs is played, and West is forced to throw the ace of diamonds. North and East both discard a heart. South plays the ace of hearts and follows with a ruff of North's last heart, squeezing East in spades and diamonds.

The hand following immediately after diagram (106), with South's ten and East's nine of spades interchanged, may be used to demonstrate the position in diagram (109).

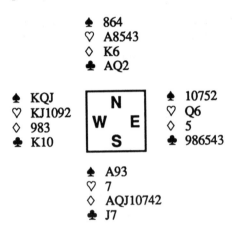

```
              ♠  864
              ♡  A8543
              ◇  K6
              ♣  AQ2

♠ KQJ        ┌─────────┐    ♠ 10752
♡ KJ1092     │    N    │    ♡ Q6
◇ 983        │ W     E │    ◇ 5
♣ K10        │    S    │    ♣ 986543
             └─────────┘
              ♠  A93
              ♡  7
              ◇  AQJ10742
              ♣  J7
```

Against South's six diamonds, West leads two rounds of spades, South's ace winning the second. At trick eight, the situation is:

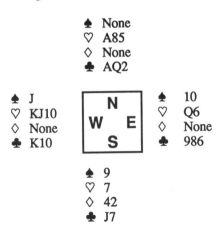

```
              ♠  None
              ♡  A85
              ◇  None
              ♣  AQ2

♠ J          ┌─────────┐    ♠ 10
♡ KJ10       │    N    │    ♡ Q6
◇ None       │ W     E │    ◇ None
♣ K10        │    S    │    ♣ 986
             └─────────┘
              ♠  9
              ♡  7
              ◇  42
              ♣  J7
```

On the lead of the four of diamonds, West is squeezed. If he discards a heart, dummy is entered with the ace of hearts and the eight of hearts can be ruffed out. If he discards the ten of clubs, the ace, jack and queen of clubs will be made in turn. And if he discards the jack of spades, North throws a heart. Now the play of the ace of hearts followed by a heart ruff squeezes East in spades and clubs.

The declarer will fail to make the contract if West switches to a heart at trick two.

Returning to diagram (109), we see that the positions of the clash menace and the one-card double menace cannot be reversed:

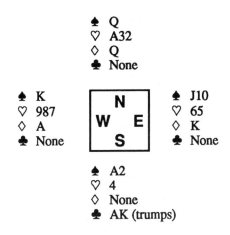

```
              ♠ Q
              ♡ A32
              ◊ Q
              ♣ None

♠ K          ┌─────────┐          ♠ J10
♡ 987        │    N    │          ♡ 65
◊ A          │  W   E  │          ◊ K
♣ None       │    S    │          ♣ None
             └─────────┘
              ♠ A2
              ♡ 4
              ◊ None
              ♣ AK (trumps)
```

The heart suit may be considered to be a three-card ruffing menace against West. As the North hand cannot be entered twice, the ruffing menace is of no value. But in this situation, if South leads a trump, West must be very careful to discard correctly. In fact, discarding in hearts is the only way to avoid conceding a trick to North-South.

(If West discards the king of spades, the queen and ace of spades will be made separately, the last trump being the entry to the South hand. If West discards the ace of diamonds, South plays another trump, North throwing two hearts, and the ace of hearts squeezes East in spades and diamonds.)

To make the position inescapable, we substitute a split three-card clash menace for the two-card clash menace in the last diagram:

(110)

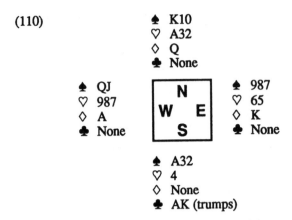

West is ruffing-clash squeezed on the lead of the ace of clubs and has to part with the ace of diamonds. North throws a heart, and East will be squeezed later on.

This is illustrated in the next hand:

Game all; IMPs; Dealer South

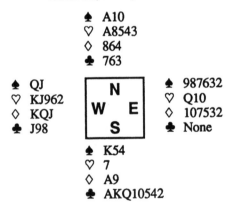

In one room the bidding was:

South	West	North	East
1♣	1♡	Double	Pass
3♣	Pass	3♡	Pass
4◊	Pass	4♠	Pass
6♣	All Pass		

In the other room, the contract was also six clubs. The two declarers received the same opening lead—the king of diamonds. One declarer won the opening lead with the ace and could not avoid going one down when the trumps proved to be 3-0. The other South player, also one down, ducked the opening lead, and won the diamond continuation. After the bad break in trumps had been revealed, he first intended to ruff a spade in dummy. When the ace of spades dropped the jack from West, he changed his plan. He led out the clubs, trying to make the contract by a double squeeze. At trick ten, he was faced with this situation:

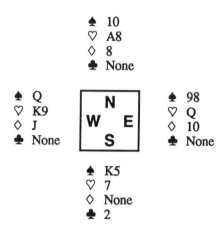

```
              ♠ 10
              ♡ A8
              ◇ 8
              ♣ None

  ♠ Q        ┌─────────┐    ♠ 98
  ♡ K9       │    N    │    ♡ Q
  ◇ J        │ W     E │    ◇ 10
  ♣ None     │    S    │    ♣ None
             └─────────┘
              ♠ K5
              ♡ 7
              ◇ None
              ♣ 2
```

South played the two of clubs, West throwing the queen of spades. Unfortunately, East held a diamond higher than dummy's eight, so the eight could not be used as a one-card menace against West. The ten and king of spades were both winners, but they could not be made separately for lack of entry.

Yet the second South player could have made the contract in a somewhat double-dummyish way. After winning the second trick with the ace of diamonds, if South plays five rounds of clubs, he arrives at a double-ruffing-clash-squeeze position similar to that of diagram (110):

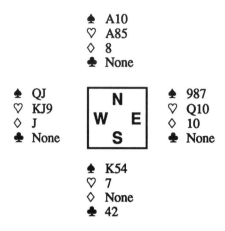

♠ A10
♥ A85
♦ 8
♣ None

♠ QJ   **N**   ♠ 987
♥ KJ9   **W E**   ♥ Q10
♦ J   **S**   ♦ 10
♣ None   ♣ None

♠ K54
♥ 7
♦ None
♣ 42

Now the four of clubs is led and West has to discard the jack of diamonds. North and East both let go of a heart. The ace of hearts is cashed, and another heart led and ruffed, squeezing East in spades and diamonds.

Diagrams (108), (109) and (110) are all non-simultaneous double positional squeezes. In each case, the clash squeeze against West operates before the simple squeeze against East.

We have seen that diagrams (108) and (109) are analogous to the single-ruffing-clash-squeeze positions in (105) and (106), respectively. The single ruffing clash squeeze in diagram (107) also has an analogue in the double ruffing clash squeeze:

(111)

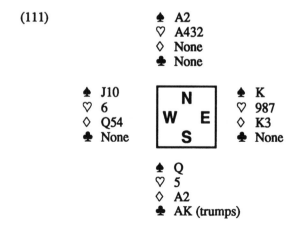

♠ A2
♥ A432
♦ None
♣ None

♠ J10   **N**   ♠ K
♥ 6   **W E**   ♥ 987
♦ Q54   **S**   ♦ K3
♣ None   ♣ None

♠ Q
♥ 5
♦ A2
♣ AK (trumps)

The ace of clubs is led, West throwing a diamond, and North a heart. East is squeezed in a ruffing-clash situation and has to unguard the diamond suit. The ace of hearts is played and a small heart led and ruffed, at which point West is squeezed in spades and diamonds.

This is an automatic double ruffing clash squeeze. The squeeze is equally effective if the East and West hands are interchanged.

It is to be noticed that in ordinary double ruffing squeezes the ruffing menace is a threat to both opponents, while in all the double-ruffing-clash-squeeze situations given above the ruffing menace is mainly against one opponent. The partner of the opponent ruffing-menaced is threatened in the suits of the clash menace and ordinary double menace. This differentiates the nature of a double ruffing clash squeeze from that of an ordinary double ruffing squeeze.

It is also to be pointed out that, in (109), (110) or (111), the partner of the opponent subjected to the ruffing clash squeeze may hold two cards in the ruffing menace suit without affecting the nature of the squeeze. When this is the case, the ruffing menace is, as we have called it, a semi-double menace.

8.7 Connections between the guard clash squeeze and the double guard squeeze

If a single guard clash squeeze were formally defined as a squeeze against one opponent in which he is threatened with a clash menace, a guard menace and an ordinary single menace, we would find immediately that such squeezes do not exist at all.

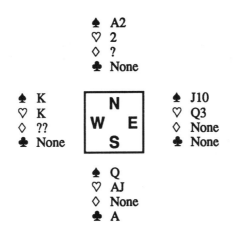

189

The spade suit is a clash menace and the heart suit a guard menace, both against West. But the two bare kings in the West hand play the same roles as two small cards, for the longer spades and hearts are both with East and a simple squeeze against East is always available for South to gain an extra trick.

Hence, should it be the case that a clash menace and a guard menace are united, then it follows that a clash squeeze would be necessary only when one opponent is clash-menaced and the other guard-menaced.

I will now discuss in detail the most interesting kind of squeeze, called the double guard clash squeeze, or simply guard clash squeeze, which is defined as a combination of a clash squeeze against one opponent and a guard squeeze against the other.

First of all, let us consider its relationship to the ordinary double guard squeezes. When one opponent is clash-menaced and the other guard-menaced, there are four possible cases, assuming that the squeeze-card is always in the South hand.

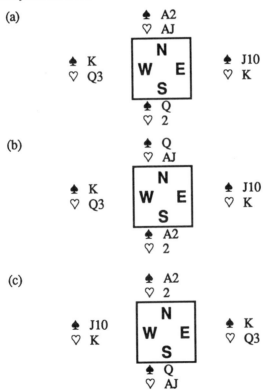

(d)

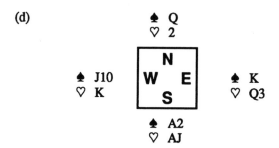

In positions (a) and (b), West is clash-menaced and East guard-menaced; in (c) and (d), the situation is reversed.

We now add to each ending an ordinary double menace and a squeeze-card to balance the holdings of the four players.

We shall try to see if any new squeeze positions can be produced. For (a):

(112)

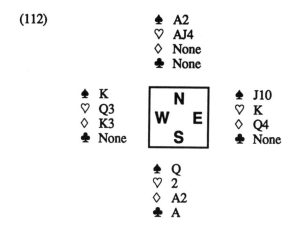

This is a guard clash squeeze with the clash squeeze against West and guard squeeze against East.

On the lead of the ace of clubs, North throws the four of hearts. If either opponent discards in a major suit, a trick will be set up in that suit; if both discard in diamonds, the two of diamonds becomes a winner.

The situation can, however, be reduced to the following ordinary simultaneous double guard squeeze if the ace of spades is played at an earlier stage.

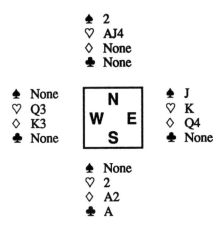

♠ 2
♡ AJ4
◇ None
♣ None

♠ None   ♠ J
♡ Q3   ♡ K
◇ K3   ◇ Q4
♣ None   ♣ None

♠ None
♡ 2
◇ A2
♣ A

When the ace of clubs is led, North discards the four of hearts. There is a guard squeeze against East and a simple squeeze against West. This is the double-guard-squeeze position in diagram (81).

But, of course, the clash menace plays an important part in diagram (112). There would be no squeeze if South held a small spade instead of the queen.

For (b), we add a split two-card double menace with the master card in the South hand in order to keep an entry to the South hand outside the clash-menace suit.

(113)

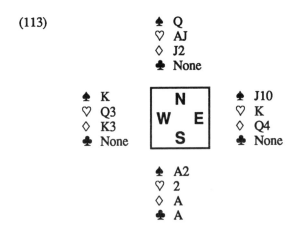

♠ Q
♡ AJ
◇ J2
♣ None

♠ K   ♠ J10
♡ Q3   ♡ K
◇ K3   ◇ Q4
♣ None   ♣ None

♠ A2
♡ 2
◇ A
♣ A

West is clash-squeezed on the lead of the ace of clubs.

The spade discard enables North's queen and South's ace of spades to be made separately. A heart discard sets up North's jack. So he has to throw a diamond. North discards the queen of spades and East is guard-squeezed.

But this guard clash squeeze is also a variation of an ordinary double guard squeeze. The spade suit need not be a clash menace and the ace of diamonds can be first played. The squeeze is equally effective even if North does not hold a card in the spade suit:

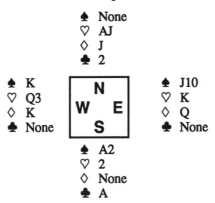

```
              ♠ None
              ♡ AJ
              ◇ J
              ♣ 2
♠ K        ┌─────────┐    ♠ J10
♡ Q3       │    N    │    ♡ K
◇ K        │ W     E │    ◇ Q
♣ None     │    S    │    ♣ None
           └─────────┘
              ♠ A2
              ♡ 2
              ◇ None
              ♣ A
```

This is the non-simultaneous double guard squeeze in diagram (79). On the lead of the ace of clubs, West throws the king of spades; East has to discard the queen of diamonds. The ace of spades then squeezes West in hearts and diamonds.

For (c):

(114)

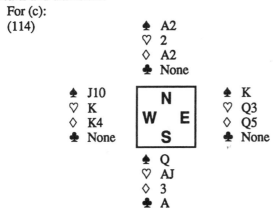

```
              ♠ A2
              ♡ 2
              ◇ A2
              ♣ None
♠ J10      ┌─────────┐    ♠ K
♡ K        │    N    │    ♡ Q3
◇ K4       │ W     E │    ◇ Q5
♣ None     │    S    │    ♣ None
           └─────────┘
              ♠ Q
              ♡ AJ
              ◇ 3
              ♣ A
```

When the ace of clubs is led, West is guard-squeezed and must discard a diamond. North lets go of the two of hearts and East is clash-squeezed.

But if the ace of spades and ace of hearts are first played, the situation is merely an ordinary double squeeze which is quite common.

It should also be pointed out that the situation in diagram (114) can be reduced to another non-simultaneous double guard squeeze if the ace of diamonds is played earlier:

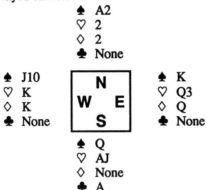

```
              ♠ A2
              ♡ 2
              ◇ 2
              ♣ None
  ♠ J10      ┌─────────┐      ♠ K
  ♡ K        │    N    │      ♡ Q3
  ◇ K        │  W   E  │      ◇ Q
  ♣ None     │    S    │      ♣ None
             └─────────┘
              ♠ Q
              ♡ AJ
              ◇ None
              ♣ A
```

On the lead of he ace of clubs, West is guard-squeezed and has to let go of the king of diamonds. North throws the two and East the king of spades. At the next trick, the ace of spades squeezes East in hearts and diamonds. The spade suit serves merely as an ordinary two-card single menace against West.

This is the non-simultaneous double guard squeeze of diagram (80).

If, in diagram (114), we replace the guard menace against West by a split three-card guard menace, we find that both North's aces can be cashed earlier in the play. The result is the fourth and final basic form of the ordinary double guard squeeze:

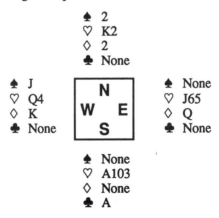

```
              ♠ 2
              ♡ K2
              ◇ 2
              ♣ None
  ♠ J        ┌─────────┐      ♠ None
  ♡ Q4       │    N    │      ♡ J65
  ◇ K        │  W   E  │      ◇ Q
  ♣ None     │    S    │      ♣ None
             └─────────┘
              ♠ None
              ♡ A103
              ◇ None
              ♣ A
```

This is the same position as diagram (82). The lead of the ace of clubs squeezes West and East simultaneously. Here the guard squeeze is against West and the simple squeeze against East.

Now for (d) we add a three-card double menace to the North hand:

(115)

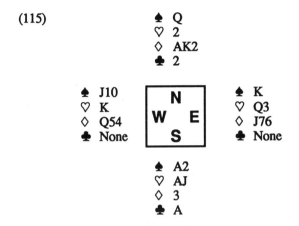

```
              ♠ Q
              ♡ 2
              ◇ AK2
              ♣ 2

  ♠ J10      ┌─────────┐      ♠ K
  ♡ K        │    N    │      ♡ Q3
  ◇ Q54      │ W     E │      ◇ J76
  ♣ None     │    S    │      ♣ None
             └─────────┘
              ♠ A2
              ♡ AJ
              ◇ 3
              ♣ A
```

When the ace of clubs is led, West is guard-squeezed and East clash-squeezed. But by first playing off the ace of spades and ace of hearts the situation again reduces to an ordinary double squeeze. The result is the simultaneous double squeeze position of diagram (19).

All the discussions, therefore, fail to give us even a single instance of the basic guard clash squeeze. But let us not be too ready to assert that such a squeeze does not exist. We shall investigate a little bit further, then we might stumble upon the real guard-clash-squeeze situations, shrouded in complexity.

8.8 Basic guard-clash-squeeze end positions

Having studied the relationship between the guard clash squeeze and the double guard squeeze, it will not be too difficult to arrive at the following situation:

(116)

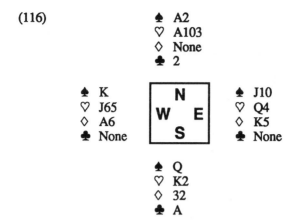

```
              ♠ A2
              ♡ A103
              ◊ None
              ♣ 2

  ♠ K                    ♠ J10
  ♡ J65      N           ♡ Q4
  ◊ A6     W   E         ◊ K5
  ♣ None     S           ♣ None

              ♠ Q
              ♡ K2
              ◊ 32
              ♣ A
```

This diagram is obtained from diagram (112) by replacing the guard menace by a split three-card guard menace and the two-card double menace by two small cards.

North-South can win four tricks out of six cards. On the lead of the ace of clubs, West and East are squeezed simultaneously: West is clash-squeezed and East is guard-squeezed. Both West and East are forced to part with a diamond. A diamond winner can then be established by conceding a trick in that suit.

In this diagram, the diamond suit in the South hand is an extended one-card double menace.

When both opponents are menaced in the other suits in which neither opponent can discard without conceding a trick, they are obliged to discard in the suit of the extended one-card double menace. The declarer can then take advantage of this in setting up an additional trick in that suit.

In diagram (116), there are two entries in the North hand and one in the South hand after the squeeze-card is played. These entries are all necessary for the gain of an extra trick. In particular, the king of hearts is the entry to cash the diamond winner, which can be established if both opponents discard in diamonds. As a consequence, the king of hearts must not be played before the ace of clubs. The ace of spades or ace of hearts must obviously not be played earlier.

A similar situation is set up if, in diagram (116), the clash menace is replaced by a split three-card clash menace and the guard menace by a two-card guard menace.

(117)

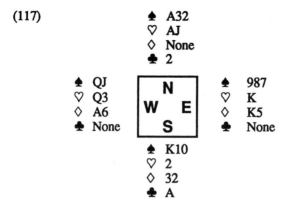

♠ A32
♡ AJ
◇ None
♣ 2

♠ QJ
♡ Q3
◇ A6
♣ None

♠ 987
♡ K
◇ K5
♣ None

♠ K10
♡ 2
◇ 32
♣ A

On the lead of the ace of clubs, West is clash-squeezed, and East guard-squeezed. Both West and East have to discard a diamond. Now a diamond lead sets up an extra winner for North-South.

In diagram (116), the positions of the clash menace and the extended double menace can be reversed. This enables us to set up another situation:

(118)

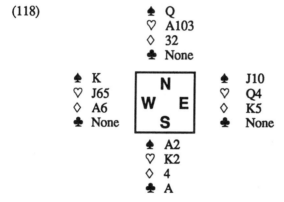

♠ Q
♡ A103
◇ 32
♣ None

♠ K
♡ J65
◇ A6
♣ None

♠ J10
♡ Q4
◇ K5
♣ None

♠ A2
♡ K2
◇ 4
♣ A

The lead of the ace of clubs forces West to throw a diamond. Since West has not discarded the king of spades, North's queen is now useless and can be thrown on the ace of clubs. At this same trick, East is guard-squeezed and must also discard a diamond. The four of diamonds is then led, conceding a trick to East-West and setting up a diamond winner in the North hand with the ace of hearts as the entry to make it.

It is clear that the clash menace is indispensable in this situation. If it is replaced by an ordinary two-card single menace against East then, on the lead of the ace of clubs, West can safely discard the king of spades and it will be impossible for South to set up a trick in the diamond suit.

Now let us examine a hand.

Love all; Dealer South

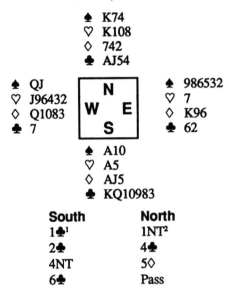

South	North
1♣[1]	1NT[2]
2♣	4♣
4NT	5◊
6♣	Pass

[1]16+ points
[2]8+ balanced

West leads the queen of spades won by South's ace. The declarer counts only eleven top tricks.

Noticing that the spade suit may possibly be used as a clash menace against West and the heart suit a split three-card guard menace against East, the declarer plays five rounds of clubs to arrive at this ending:

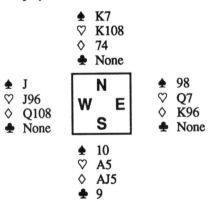

If the ace of diamonds is cashed, the situation will be the same as in diagram (116). On the lead of the nine of clubs, both West and East are forced to discard in diamonds. Now the lead of a diamond establishes a trick for South who makes a total of twelve tricks and the contract.

Diagrams (116) to (118) are simultaneous guard clash squeezes with the clash squeeze against West and guard squeeze against East. Our last four situations are guard clash squeezes with the clash squeeze against East and guard squeeze against West.

The first is this:

(119)

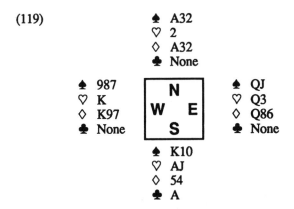

```
            ♠ A32
            ♡ 2
            ◊ A32
            ♣ None
♠ 987     ┌─────────┐   ♠ QJ
♡ K       │    N    │   ♡ Q3
◊ K97     │  W   E  │   ◊ Q86
♣ None    │    S    │   ♣ None
          └─────────┘
            ♠ K10
            ♡ AJ
            ◊ 54
            ♣ A
```

The spade suit in the North-South hands is a split three-card clash menace against East, the heart suit is a guard menace against West, and the diamond suit is an extended two-card double menace.

The lead of the ace of clubs squeezes West, who has to discard a diamond. North lets go of the two of hearts, and East is clash-squeezed and must also discard a diamond. A diamond winner is established after conceding a trick in that suit.

The following two situations are similar to that of diagram (119):

(120)

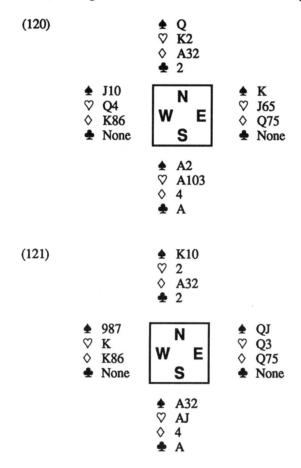

♠ Q
♥ K2
♦ A32
♣ 2

♠ J10   **N**   ♠ K
♥ Q4   **W**   **E**   ♥ J65
♦ K86   **S**   ♦ Q75
♣ None   ♣ None

♠ A2
♥ A103
♦ 4
♣ A

(121)

♠ K10
♥ 2
♦ A32
♣ 2

♠ 987   **N**   ♠ QJ
♥ K   **W**   **E**   ♥ Q3
♦ K86   **S**   ♦ Q75
♣ None   ♣ None

♠ A32
♥ AJ
♦ 4
♣ A

In diagrams (120) and (121), both West and East have to shorten their diamond holdings on the lead of the ace of clubs and a trick can then be set up for North-South in that suit.

In these diagrams, the spade suit is a clash menace against East, the heart suit is a guard menace against West, and the diamond suit is an extended two-card double menace.

It is easily seen that the ace of diamonds cannot be played earlier; a diamond must be led from the South hand after both opponents have discarded a diamond on the lead of the ace of clubs.

We give another example hand in which the contract can be made by performing a guard clash squeeze.

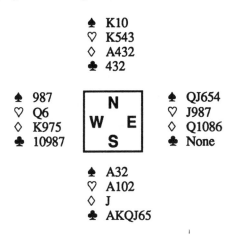

```
          ♠ K10
          ♡ K543
          ◇ A432
          ♣ 432
♠ 987              ♠ QJ654
♡ Q6               ♡ J987
◇ K975             ◇ Q1086
♣ 10987            ♣ None
          ♠ A32
          ♡ A102
          ◇ J
          ♣ AKQJ65
```

South is declarer at six no-trumps and the opening lead is the ten of clubs, which South wins. The declarer plays three more rounds of clubs, leaving this situation:

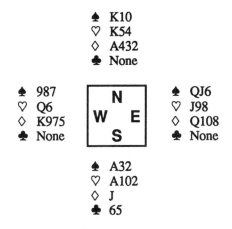

```
          ♠ K10
          ♡ K54
          ◇ A432
          ♣ None
♠ 987              ♠ QJ6
♡ Q6               ♡ J98
◇ K975             ◇ Q108
♣ None             ♣ None
          ♠ A32
          ♡ A102
          ◇ J
          ♣ 65
```

The declarer still has two losers, but he cannot afford to concede an early trick to rectify the count. The heart suit may be used as a guard menace against West, but the spades and diamonds are protected by both opponents.

The six of clubs is therefore played, West and North both throwing a diamond. East is forced to discard in spades or diamonds. If he discards a spade, the position becomes:

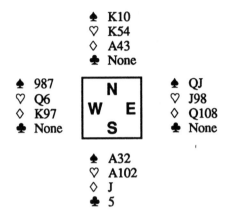

♠ K10
♡ K54
◇ A43
♣ None

♠ 987   ♠ QJ
♡ Q6   ♡ J98
◇ K97   ◇ Q108
♣ None   ♣ None

♠ A32
♡ A102
◇ J
♣ 5

The five of clubs is now led, North discarding a heart. Both opponents have to part with a diamond. An extra diamond winner can then be set up for South by first conceding a trick in that suit. The situation is similar to those of diagrams (120) and (121).

Returning to the nine-card position above, if East discards a diamond on the six of clubs, the declarer plays the five of clubs and again a heart is discarded from dummy. If West now lets go of a diamond, the declarer makes the contract as before. And if West retains the length in diamonds by unguarding the spade suit, East has to throw another diamond. The jack of diamonds is then led and ducked, allowing either opponent to win. When North regains the lead, the ace of diamonds is played and East is caught in a positional simple squeeze in spades and hearts.

The contract can be made against best defence provided the opening lead is not a diamond. Problem solvers may note that the hand develops into various squeeze endings.

In the eight-card position above, East having reduced his spade holding to queen-jack alone, we see that the extended two-card double menace may be replaced by an extended one-card double menace. This enables us to set up another basic seven-card end position of the guard clash squeeze.

(122)

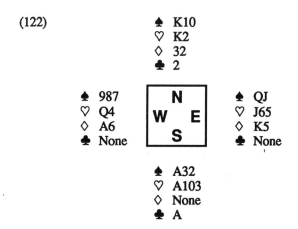

```
                 ♠ K10
                 ♡ K2
                 ◇ 32
                 ♣ 2

  ♠ 987          ┌───────┐          ♠ QJ
  ♡ Q4           │   N   │          ♡ J65
  ◇ A6           │ W   E │          ◇ K5
  ♣ None         │   S   │          ♣ None
                 └───────┘

                 ♠ A32
                 ♡ A103
                 ◇ None
                 ♣ A
```

On the lead of the ace of clubs, West is guard-squeezed, and East clash-squeezed. The North hand can be entered twice: once to lead a diamond after both opponents have discarded in diamonds, and a second time to cash the established diamond winner.

It might appear that the guard clash squeeze is too difficult to handle, since in actual play it would be hardly possible for a declarer to place exact cards with one opponent and the rest with the other. But often a contract is made by planning the play on the assumption that the right cards are dealt to the right opponent. To learn and understand all the basic situations would doubtlessly enable us to fulfill many seemingly unmakeable contracts in our lifetime of play. It is also possible to construct many of the most beautiful and complicated "against any defence" double-dummy problems on the basis of the guard-clash-squeeze diagrams.

I have now given all the clash-squeeze situations I was able to work out. I make no claims of completeness, but I think the fundamental forms are all there.

A single clash squeeze is reducible to either a simple squeeze or to a double clash squeeze. The ruffing clash squeeze and guard clash squeeze are very rarely met in play and not easily recognised. It is the double-clash-squeeze positions that I believe will become important and applicable in practice. Our playing ability is continually advancing, and some day we may find every bridge player executing a double clash squeeze as easily as we make a simple throw-in nowadays.